151 - Masturbation!
151 - dangers of sex & mast
152 - insanity & mast

156 - contraceptives
156 - Prost - cannot get pregnant

P. 68 - abortion
68 - prostitute

P. 69 - contra-
157 ceptive
P. 78 - Venus
(aphrodite)
- april 23
86 - in graves
88 - Plato on
Venus
98 - Religion & sex
99 - christianity
101 - clothes
103/4 Church
against sex

141 - homosex
142 - turn-ons
189 - 147 - "porn
149 - Baptist
Register
174 - words
175 - "
179 - 70% in
jail

186 - VD

189 - incest
prostitute

SEX AND SUPERSTITION

SEX AND SUPERSTITION

G. L. Simons

ABELARD-SCHUMAN
London

First published 1973
ISBN 0 200 71959 9

LONDON
Abelard-Schuman
Limited,
450 Edgeware Road
W2

AYLESBURY
Abelard-Schuman
Limited
24 Market Square
Aylesbury, Bucks

Printed in Great Britain by
Willmer Brothers Limited, Birkenhead

CONTENTS

Prodigies, omens, oracles, judgements quite obscure the few natural events that are intermingled with them. But as the former grow thinner every page, in proportion as we advance nearer the enlightened times, we soon learn, that there is nothing mysterious or supernatural in the case, but that all proceeds from the usual propensity of mankind towards the marvellous; and that though this inclination may at intervals receive a check from sense and learning, it can never be thoroughly extirpated from human nature.

David Hume (1711–76)

INTRODUCTION

Some people see widespread superstition as inevitable, some even regard it as desirable. Kenneth Mather, a geneticist, has suggested that if it supports a social norm beneficial to a human group it may be seen as having positive survival value (*Human Diversity*, 1964). And Gustav Jahoda (*The Psychology of Superstition*, 1970) has little sympathy with the notion of superstition as *error*. Such anthropologists as Margaret Mead and Lévi-Strauss have shown that superstition in primitive society is often a complex and goal-serving phenomenon. In such a view, superstition can be seen as meeting important needs in human psychology.

At worst, superstition leads to excessive cruelty, a harsh indifference to human interest: at best it may protect a vulnerable psychology (it may also cause it). At all times it represents a suspension of the faculty for rational criticism, a clutching at easy answers (and ones convivial to existing moral prejudice). Superstition, as irrationalism, is a poor substitute for sober reflection.

In sexual attitudes superstition has much to answer for. Virgins have been sacrificed to merciless gods. Bizarre operations have been performed to restore lost potency. Children have been mutilated in the name of virtue. And adult men and women have been executed for harmless sexual indulgence. When people talk of superstition they generally do not recollect such things. In modern times the most bizarre cruelties no longer exist, but cruelty endures—nakedly in primitive society, less obviously in the developed world: in pressurizing unmarried mothers to be aborted against their wishes, in sustaining punitive legislation against harmless sexual behaviour, in introducing sexual guilt and tension in young people by poisoning in a thousand ways their sexual attitudes.

One purpose of the present book is to show the continuity of sexual superstition in human society. Emphases, priorities and preoccupations change. Some trends are arrested or diverted. The objects of superstition are replaced by others. But always the props of superstition remain—the irrational anxieties, the primitive taboo-responses, the essential ritual, the neurotic ethical vigour. In areas of fact and humanity we are perhaps improving. It is easier to obtain accurate information on sex, and an increasing number of people are sympathetic to the sexual predicament. At the same time the forces of superstition are mustering, as they always will in reaction. They may only be fighting a rearguard action. If their efforts amount to more than this then the way to sexual liberation, emancipation from neurotic guilt, freedom from taboo, is blocked, and human happiness will have to wait.

CHAPTER ONE

THE NATURE OF SUPERSTITION

People don't mind knocking on wood or throwing salt over their shoulder but at the same time they feel a bit silly when asked about why they do it. And they will not call their more fundamental beliefs—on, say, God or sexual morality —*superstitious.* Rather they will talk of them as *rational, informed, mature.*

> Without tearing out the hearts of human sacrificial victims on a high altar we cannot be sure the sun will rise tomorrow (daily Aztec practice)

> The disasters following sexual intercourse with a nursing mother can only be averted by performing complex rituals including cutting off the ear of a dog (according to the religion of the Nuer reported by Evans-Pritchard)

> By talking Latin or the vernacular to biscuit and wine we can turn them into the flesh and blood of a dead Semite (orthodox Roman Catholicism)

In one important sense these beliefs seem very similar involving a mysterious cause-effect relationship that people have employed—or still do—though not understanding it. Today most of us in the developed West would dismiss the first two examples but many people would hedge about the third. All we need remark is that superstition is partly a subjective matter, at once absurdity to some and important commitment to others.

The word *superstition* derives from the Latin *superstitio* —the term used by Tacitus to denote the alien beliefs and practices of the early Christians. This in turn comes from the verb *stare* and is the equivalent of the English *survival,* the French *survivance,* and the German *Überbleibsel.* An important feature of superstition is its capacity to persist from one generation to the next despite a whole range of hostile pressures: in this sense superstition has continuity and can be distinguished from today's new widespread but irrational belief.

In its inception superstition sprang from man's helplessness in the face of Nature. He created ritual and taboo to shield him from the hostile forces all around; magic, almost akin to science in its purpose, became the key to an understanding of natural processes; and religion the means to propitiation of vindictive supernatural agencies that operated everywhere. Superstitious belief thus became a tool for handling the natural and supernatural world, a device to allow people to carry on the affairs of daily life.

Superstitious belief has a number of features that can be identified. *Omens,* for instance—the signs and warnings about the future—are a frequent component of superstition. Finding a pin on the ground is an omen of good luck, as is a dog following you home; an itchy ear is an omen of misfortune. Alexander Krappe[1] divides omens into two classes— according to whether or not they have featured in a major religious system. A religious searching for omens has taken place in such activities as ornithomancy (studying, for example, the flight of birds), haruspicy (examining the entrails of animals), incubation (sleeping in a holy place to receive a nocturnal visitation from a divinity), hydromancy (divination by water), and astrology, In all such activities priests have officiated to impress the laity and so preserve the priest-class as a privileged élite.

The ancient Romans developed a system of augury (from *avis,* bird, thus meaning divination by studying birds, or soothsaying in general). Throughout the Middle Ages augury had a powerful hold in Spain and Southern France. The *Poema de Milo Cid* narrates how its hero pays attention to the croakings of the crow, and an old collection of Italian *novelle* describes a nobleman who, "like most of his countrymen," is addicted to practices of augury.

Haruspicy (from the Assyrian *har* meaning liver) originated in Babylonia and was carried West by the Etruscan priesthood. Divination from the shoulder-blades or the "wishbone" of fowl is still a popular superstition in Europe and elsewhere.

The practice of incubation was widespread in the ancient world. The advent of Christianity did not put a stop to it: people simply slept in Christian churches instead of in pagan temples. And incubation has been found in many primitive tribes. The person is sometimes given a drug, after which, during sleep, the divine revelation is virtually assured. Even today, in some rural areas of Europe, concoctions of herbs and flowers are placed under the pillow and thought to have the power to stimulate illuminating dreams.

Hydromancy was closely connected with the worship of sacred wells and springs. This too was common in antiquity.

Divination by means of the spirits of the dead, termed *necromancy*, is a precursor of modern spiritualism, and was practiced in ancient Greece, Arabic lands and various parts of medieval Europe. The oldest known example is the *Nekyia* of the Odyssey. The tale of the Witch of Endor, Othin's conjuration of the dead *volva* in the Norse *Voluspa*, and a story forming part of the *Hervarar Saga* show how widespread the doctrine has been.

Of all the omen-searching techniques, past and current, perhaps astrology has the biggest literature. The early astrologers amassed much information on the movements of the planets and the positions of the "fixed" stars, and it is likely that their efforts laid the basis for serious astronomy and such early achievements as the prediction of eclipses. In the main, however, astrology, like alchemy, has been left behind by the rigours of scientific method. By its nature astrology could not evolve. Krappe, writing in 1930, complained of the "conservatism" of "planetary books"—they "reveal essentially the same axioms and reasonings which made up ancient astrology and which were still believed in in Cromwell's time."

In addition to the ritualized search for omens as part of religious practice there exist the simple folk beliefs concerning everyday signs and forewarnings. Thus an old woman signifies ill luck, partly because of the sterility associated with her person. Sometimes women are seen as representing a generalized danger and men in some primitive societies try to steer clear of them before setting out on a hunting or fishing expedition. The priest of the Church in Old Ireland, regarded as the "weak man," was similarly tainted and to encounter him when engaged upon a manly pursuit was thought to bode ill.

Omens can be found in all spheres of human experience. In weather-lore, for example, rain at a funeral generally means that the corpse is "blessed;" a medieval Icelandic story relates how a good man whose funeral was accompanied by storm was rewarded by eternal bliss, whilst his wicked wife had sunshine at her funeral and went to hell. Another Icelandic tale, as part of animal-lore, tells of a young girl who avoids danger by being warned in time by a raven. In tree-lore the ash is thought to have particular power against witchcraft, a belief connected with Pliny's famous comment about the aversion of snakes for ash-trees: some plants—Irish shamrock and the ringwort of Apuleius— offer protection against the evil eye.

Closely related to the concept of omen is the notion of *taboo*. The anthropologist Sir James Frazer compared taboo with an electrical insulator. People in various critical situations and circumstances—children at birth, menstruating women, men on their death-bed—are charged with a mysterious force which is powerful and all-pervasive. Correctly handled it can be rendered harmless and even turned to good effect, like electricity. But at the same time people need to be shielded from its power. This is the purpose of taboo. In primitive society taboos are numerous; in developed society less so but still detectable. The inadvisability of walking under a ladder, breaking a mirror and upsetting salt are obvious cases in point. Taboo is less concerned with propitiation of supernatural intelligences (though the desire not to provoke evil spirits has played a part) than with an understanding of the blind and mysterious forces that operate in Nature. Thus traditional taboo is principally concerned with magic.

Frazer[2] divided sympathetic magic into two principal classes—homoeopathic (or imitative) and contagious. In homoeopathic magic, wizards or laymen attempt to achieve desired results by using images or models, or by imitating in action an event to be realized. The underlying principle is that of like producing like. The Peruvian Indians used to mould images of fat mixed with grain to represent people they hated or feared, and then burned the effigy on the road where the intended victim was to pass. A Malay technique was to take spittle, nail-parings, hair and so forth from the intended victim, make them into his likeness with wax from a deserted bees' comb, and scorch the figure slowly for seven nights. (This Malay ruse also employs the *contagious* principle —see below).

When, among the Dyaks of Borneo, a woman is in hard labour a wizard in an adjoining room assists by pretending to be an expectant mother: a large stone tied to his stomach represents the baby in the womb, and following directions shouted to him by a colleague attending the mother, he moves the make-believe baby about until the real infant is born. The process of adoption has often been accompanied by make-believe childbirth. Thus in parts of Bulgaria a woman will take a boy whom she intends to adopt and pull him through her clothes to make the maternal bond complete. In ancient Greece, if a man thought to be dead survived, it was necessary for him to be reborn: he was passed through a woman's lap, washed, dressed in swaddling clothes, and put out to nurse. In ancient India, in similar circumstances, a man had to pass a night in a tub filled with fat and water; there he was obliged to sit, silent and with doubled-up fists, like a child in the womb.

Homoeopathic magic was also used to cure or prevent sickness. The ancient Hindus aimed to cure jaundice by banishing the yellow colour to yellow creatures and yellow things. As the appropriate spell was intoned the patient was given water to drink mixed with the hair of a red bull so that he might take on a more healthy colour.

Contagious magic is based on the idea that whatever has been once joined must remain so for ever. Anything done to a part of a person will affect the person himself. Thus, in primitive society, when a child loses a tooth it must be guarded lest it be eaten by an animal or acquired by an enemy.

Certain tribes in Western Australia believed that a man would swim well or not, according to whether his mother at his birth threw his navel-string into water. Natives of Queensland used to believe that part of a child's spirit stays in the afterbirth: the grandmother buried the afterbirth so that Anjea, the being who causes women to conceive, could retrieve the spirit for use in a new baby.

Another element in contagious magic is the peculiar relationship that is thought to exist between a wounded man and the thing that wounded him. Pliny remarks that if you have wounded a man and are sorry for it, the pain of the sufferer will be instantly alleviated if you spit on the hand that gave the wound. In Melanesia, if a man can keep the arrow that wounded him in a cool place, the inflammation of the wound will die away: at the same time the enemy who inflicted the wound is striving to make it worse by keeping the bow that caused it close to the fire.

In some societies it was thought that if you drive a nail into a man's footprint he would instantly become lame: a maxim ascribed to Pythagoras forbids such action. The aborigines of Victoria used to put hot embers in the tracks of animals to make their escape impossible; Thompson Indians used to put charms on the tracks of a wounded deer to make it die quickly.

Closely associated with such practices is the concept of *ritual*. It is not enough that action be taken; it has to be carried out in a precise fashion. In simple societies the rituals are complex and involve lengthy preparation. Modern Western society is not all that different. Few of us are contemptuous of wedding ceremonies or the rituals surrounding infant baptism, funerals or coronations.

Much of the impulse to superstitious belief springs from fear of the unknown. Alexander Krappe sees the fear-of-the-unknown doctrine as not quite the right emphasis and prefers "fear of the abnormal" as the motivation behind superstition. It is argued that the heavenly eclipse—the abnormal event—is what stirs up the superstitious dread, not the normal procession of planets across the sky. An eclipse was seen as a fierce monster about to swallow up the heavenly bodies; and so the folk beneath tried to frighten it away by making an infernal noise—a ruse that always worked.

In more mundane matters the abnormal can be detected in such things as twin births, albinos and idiots. In many primitive regions the mother of twins and her offspring were destroyed and the hut in which the birth had taken place was razed to prevent all contagion. Part of the trouble stemmed from the erroneous belief that each of the twins had a different father, leading to the idea that the mother was guilty of adultery. In the same harsh spirit, albinos have been put to death in savage societies all over the world. Idiots have generally met with a happier fate, often being viewed in primitive communities with veneration and regarded as prophets and seers. Blindness has been afforded similar esteem, and there were many blind seers in Ancient Greece—for example, Kassandra, Helenos and Teiresias.

It has also been suggested that fear of the *evil eye* derived from actual malformations of the human eye: thus in Mediterranean countries the evil eye is regarded as in general a blue eye, whilst in the North of Europe it is thought to be black. People whose eyebrows meet have been regarded with great suspicion. In parts of Europe such people were thought to be werewolves; in the Balkans they are thought to be vampires after death.

It is generally the case that as societies become more sophisticated they tend to become less superstitious, at least where their superstition has an explicit reference to super-natural phenomena. We will see in Chapter Six how super-

B

stition can be preserved in secular society; but at the same time we have to acknowledge that its character has changed. We no longer have the gross superstition that was a principal feature of medieval Europe. At such a time the world was thought to contain witches, wizards, demons, devils and all manner of strange beasts; medical practice was accompanied by magical incantation; and supernatural intervention by both God and evil spirits was thought to be commonplace. We no longer see things in quite the same way, and a whole range of superstition and credulity has passed into disrepute, at least in much of the developed world.

Conversely, beliefs dubbed *superstitious* may come to be widely accepted. Just before the turn of the century a book was published with the title *Studies of Contemporary Superstition*[3] in which the author attacked the current laws on marriage and divorce, Fabian socialism, and the agnosticism of T. H. Huxley. He called agnosticism "a superstition more abject, more meaningless, and more ridiculous than that of any African savage, grovelling and mumbling before his fetish." As soon as people with committed beliefs come into contact with foreign cultures they invent a facile device for dismissing such cultures, of maintaining the superiority of their own creeds. Thus writers on superstition usually feel obliged to distinguish it from *true* religion. *Superstition* is generally defined in terms of *false worship* or *irrational belief in supernatural phenomena*. Thus the anthropologist Malinowski[4] asks—*Has primitive man a religion? Or is he merely obsessed by savage superstitions, surrounded by the darkness of heathendom?* Douglas Hill[5] talks of superstition as an "illegitimate branch of religious history." And Robert Graves, writing in the introduction of the Larousse Encyclopedia of Mythology, notes of myth that *Mythology is the study of ... legends ... so foreign to a student's experience that he cannot believe them to be true*. For the true believer there is a paradox, noted by Graves and others, that is difficult to resolve—namely that Biblical narratives are closely paralleled by myths from Persia, Babylonia, Egypt, Greece and other ancient cultures.

People worry lest superstition be detected in their own

religion: perhaps there is not true and false religion but only superstition. One heroic but shortsighted way out of the dilemma is to make the whole thing a semantic matter. Thus Krappe proposes that it would be best "to define as *superstition* any belief or practice that is not recommended or enjoined by any of the great organized religions such as Christianity, Judaism, Islam, and Buddhism." The explorer Sir Richard Burton observed sardonically that the very same missionaries who objected to the native's use of magic teeth, bones and wizard's mats recommended in their stead relics, medals and consecrated palm leaves.[6]

We are now in a position to identify the two central questions about superstition. These may be termed the *psychological* and the *epistemological*: the first concerns *why* people come to believe in superstitious doctrines, the second concerns the relationship of superstition to rationality and truth.

In both primitive and developed society the belief in fate/luck/fortune/chance persists: it is thought that a mysterious world underlies the physical world and is capable of interacting with it. Once the superstition has been created and made widespread there are powerful social reasons making for its survival. People learn, i.e. they soak up their culture. The few folk who are able to stand outside their culture and survey it critically have, on one view, strong independent minds, or, from another angle, a degree of social maladjustment that amounts to sickness. All societies have evolved techniques for dealing with rebels and mental cases.

Psycho-analysts and others sympathetic to the Freudian schema of personality see superstition as being generated by the subconscious. William James, in *The Varieties of Religious Experience,* denoted "full sunlit consciousness" the A-region of personality to distinguish it from the B-region. This latter he saw as the greater part of each of us, the abode of all things latent, "the reservoir of everything that passes unrecorded or unobserved." Furthermore it is the wellspring of our passions and prejudices—*our intuitions, hypotheses, fancies, superstitions, persuasions, convictions, and in general all our non-rational operations, come from it.* The clear implication is that we do not contrive a superstition through ratiocination, as we may a scientific hypothesis.

A patient of Freud once related to him what she thought had been a prophetic dream about meeting the family doctor.[7] When she went to town she met him where she had dreamt she would. Upon examination it was found that she had no recollection of the dream before actually meeting the doctor. Freud concluded that it was probably during the course of the meeting that she had acquired the conviction of having had the dream. Subsequent analysis showed that the woman had been attached to a friend of the doctor, and that the friend had failed to keep a date the day before the supposed dream. Freud's interpretation of the woman's experience runs thus—". . . her illusion, when she saw her friend of former days, of having had a prophetic dream was equivalent to some such remark as this: 'Ah, doctor, you remind me now of past times, when I never had to wait in vain for N if we'd arranged a meeting.' "

In *Totem and Taboo* Freud traces back the conviction in certain people that their thoughts are omnipotent, i.e. that if they think unkind thoughts about a person, for example, he will soon die or fall ill. Freud traces the idea back to the sexual development of early childhood: during a narcissistic phase the capacity of one's own psychic processes to affect the outer world is greatly overestimated. The Freudian Ferenczi has pointed out that the gestures and crying of the baby do in fact achieve their object, leading the infant to feel that it controls the outside world. Freud himself believed that the persistence of the narcissistic phase was a feature of primitive peoples and could serve as an explanation for their magical beliefs.

A number of Freudians have written about superstitious belief. Robert Fliess,[8] discussed by Jahoda, views it as a prototype of a magical ritual. Particular attention is given to the superstitious practice of "knocking on wood." Fliess begins by stating that "the individual is forced to perform this ritual by a fearful tension, produced by the anticipation of aggression at the hands of 'fate' (formerly the parents)." This view does not entirely satisfy him and he looks for an explanation at a deeper psychic layer, going back to the pre-oedipal period in infancy. According to Fliess—wood = mother, finger = penis, and three (from the three traditional knocks) = male genitalia. In the words of Fliess:

> She, the mother (womb), is approached from below, and with an ambivalent attitude towards castration: the subject's own phallic genital is denied (the bent finger) and at the same time affirmed (the three knocks). The "knocking" itself can only be an intended destruction and impregnation.

A later paper by Judd Marmor,[9] another Freudian, covers similar ground. He considers why well-educated people in the twentieth century feel compelled to perform, albeit sheepishly, semi-magical rituals such as "knocking on wood." The answer is that most men have never outgrown the characterization of "fate," the Christian "God," or the classical "gods" as parent surrogates. And the anxiety generated by a consciousness of an all-pervasive authority has to be dissipated through ritual.

Where Freud and other tough-minded pychologists have been predictably hostile to superstition, assuming its falsity, Jung has been altogether more sympathetic to superstitious belief. He refused to make firm distinctions between true and false belief, and preferred to emphasize the functions that superstition performs in human life. Above all he worried that modern man was becoming a slave to "materialist dogmas" and thought it significant that primitive peoples remain fully alive to both the physical and spiritual worlds, taking spirits as direct evidence of spiritual reality. In his autobiographical work he gives many examples of experiences, particularly prophetic dreams, which he believes are evidence for a spiritual world. With the growth of modern behaviourism superstition came to be regarded as a conditioned response. Skinner has pointed out that whereas the bulk of conditioning aids personal and social survival—as for example where the child who has burnt its fingers fears the boiling kettle—there are instances of "accidental" stimuli where conditioning irrelevant to survival can be set up. Thus a child fearing contact with *all* dogs, whether harmless or not, through a solitary unhappy experience, would be acting irrationally.

Pressing the point that conditioning can operate equally with animals and humans, Skinner wrote a systematic exposition with the unlikely title—" 'Superstition' in the pigeon."[10] A pigeon was placed in a cage in which food appeared when the bird performed in a certain way, the particular behaviour to be encouraged ("reinforced") not being selected by the experimentors but being left to chance. Thus one pigeon happened to turn it head counterclockwise at the crucial time; the reinforcement strengthened the response and it came to be performed more frequently than other responses. In due course a kind of ritual turning came to be established. With another pigeon a particular kind of head movement was singled out, but in some cases an insufficient number of fortuitous linkages occurred to produce a "superstition." Skinner notes that, "The bird behaves as if there were a causal relation between its behaviour and the presentation of food." This underlines the point already made—that much superstition hinges on a mistaken view of causal connections. Skinner suggests that the principle operating with the experimental pigeons applies also in the formulation of human superstition. The idea is developed in *Science and Human Behaviour*.[11]

Skinner argues that the fewer the reinforcements required to alter the probability of a response, the greater the risk that a mere coincidence will result in a superstition. It is conceded that in the process of social transmission a number of other factors, in particular the verbal element, need to be considered.

Jahoda objects that the theory makes inadequate distinction between *irrational* belief or behaviour and *superstition,* and points to a central confusion in Skinner's work on superstition—the failure to distinguish between (*a*) behaviour induced by the accidental sequence of response and reinforcement and (*b*) the belief that a casual connection is involved.

Without the belief being present it is hard to see that superstition could exist.

John Whiting, a psychological anthropologist influenced by both Freudian and behaviourist theory, conducted a field study among a New Guinea tribe with the object, in part, of examining the social transmission of supernatural beliefs. Among these are beliefs in ghosts, sorcery and great monsters called *marsalai*. Whiting believes that the beliefs are inculcated by a generalization from real dangers, where *generalization* means a conditioned response to a stimulus which only resembles the conditioned stimulus in certain respects. A distinction is drawn between the realistic and unrealistic warnings issued by "teachers," those persons charged with the task of guiding and controlling the young. Realistic warnings are ones which, if ignored, lead to pain, e.g. avoidance of poisonous foods, respect for the property of others, girls not to behave immodestly: an unrealistic warning is one where no unpleasant consequences will follow non-observance. The overall result is that a habit of observing warnings is created, which extends to non-existent dangers.

A later work deals with the fear of ghosts at funeral ceremonies.[12] The social role of supernatural sanctions is outlined and the particular question of why the feared ghosts are likely to be those of one's parents is examined. Whiting asks *what are the child-rearing conditions that should lead to a preoccupation with parental ghosts?* The answer is that the child, conscious of its needs, is likely to fantasize about its parents satisfying these needs. When the mother comes to attend to him the act should "reinforce his magical thinking and increase the probability that he will produce fantasy images of his mother when she is absent and he is in need." *It is our hypothesis that this type of magical thinking underlies a preoccupation with ghosts and spirits.* A ramification of the doctrine is that in societies where a child's needs are met immediately fear of ghosts ought to be low; and conversely where children are left in distress for some time, it ought to be high.

In summary we can note that all interpretations, even Jung's, assume at least a broadly systematic response of the individual to his social and personal situation. Superstition becomes a mechanism to lubricate his transactions with other people and the general problems of life in society.

One definition of superstition is in terms of ignorant and irrational belief in supernatural agency. The idea of ignorance implies the absence of information crucial to the formulation of reasonable opinion. (It is in this spirit that Bertrand Russell advanced a "wildly paradoxical and subversive" doctrine—that it is undesirable to believe a proposition *when there is no ground whatever for supposing it true.*)[13] The importance of information (evidence) in arriving at true propositions has always been emphasized by philosophers with a rationalist bent. It is hard to see how anyone could object, at least in principle, to such a view. What it entails is that there are objective standards whereby truth can be distinguished from falsehood, and that superstitious belief arises when men are ignorant of these standards or choose not to observe them.

The commonsense view is that the world has certain features and characteristics, and that knowledge consists in apprehending what these features are: superstition consists in building up a false image of what the world is really like. In philosophy the doctrine is sometimes called the *correspondence* theory of truth, our statements being factual (or in error) to the extent that they mirror (or do not) the reality they aim to describe.

The aim of the scientific approach to truth is to apply standards which can be relied upon to assign at least a degree of probability to particular propositions. The approach serves to generate a definition of superstition. Thus A. E. Heath in the 1948 *Rationalist Annual,*

The point I wish to stress is that superstition, whether casual or not, can be treated on objective lines. It is a mathematical matter of the odds for or against. This provides a rough "ready-reckoner" for assigning beliefs to their proper place on a scale stretching from mere superstition to reasonable expectation.[14]

It is important to appreciate that this approach can be applied to orthodox religious belief—

> If there is evidence for a belief, if its probabilities are calculable and of reasonable amount, then there is nothing irrational in taking a chance in believing it. But if the odds cannot be estimated, or if they are grossly weighted against what is believed, then the belief is a superstition. It's a gambler's throw, which can readily crystallize about itself all the paraphernalia of superstition—amulets, charms, and sacred relics.

The Danish psychologist Alfred Lehmann viewed superstition as error. In his book *Superstition and Magic*[15] he provides a historical account of magical and superstitious beliefs, and offers also a psychological analysis of what he terms the "magical states of mind." Lehmann ran mockseances on an experimental basis, devising a number of magical tricks which he called "psychic phenomena" to capture the interest of his subjects. It was shown that the people involved in the experiment—including scholars, businessmen and journalists—were liable to certain forms of error in perception. Thus a superstition could be created by errors of observation (reference to unicorns, the giant snakes described by Pliny, etc). In a more indirect way, bias could enter into the observation to distort it. Thus with comets already regarded as portents it is not suprising that people imagined they saw them as burning beams, flaming swords, dragons and other weird spectacles. Similarly there could be errors of memory: events confirming predictions are cited as confirmation, whilst other events are forgotten. Lehmann concludes his work with the comment—"All the superstitious beliefs, whose natural context we tried to demonstrate here, were at the beginning only false interpretations of phenomena more or less inadequately observed."

There is a general consensus of opinion that semantic understanding in the child arises through its early experience of the (physical) world: its concept of meaning comes to be based on a range of empirical data supplied through its senses. If this is the genesis of meaningful discourse it is difficult to see what the word *supernatural* could signify, if in fact we intend it to relate to something totally different in kind to the rest of the natural reality. An example may clarify the point: a primitive society ignorant of wireless may regard a transistor radio as a supernatural device. From their point of view they would be quite right to do so, and the argument can be generalized. In such an interpretation the supernatural is simply *a part of the physical world not yet fully understood.*

Some people, conscious of the ritual element in much superstitious behaviour, suggest that true superstition embodies both a theoretical system of belief and a set of accompanying activities. This is certainly true of much ancient and modern superstition, but again it may be unwise to press the point. There is a sense in which *all* belief has the capacity to influence action *given the appropriate circumstances.* For a belief to be acknowledged as superstitious it does not need to have an active corollary *at that time.* It is enough that the belief in question incline people to certain behaviour in a given social or personal context. Since *all* belief has this capacity we are emphasizing in the present work the theoretical aspect of superstition rather than the ritual aspect, i.e. while we will give many instances of what people *do* in their superstitious moods we will be more concerned with the beliefs that underlie the behaviour.

My main concern is with erroneous belief—supernatural or not, widespread or not, and associated with ritual or not. In particular I am concerned with erroneous beliefs, past and present, in the field of sexual attitudes. *Superstition* seems a good word to use—much in the way that Bertrand Russell talked of "superstitious ethics,"[16] i.e. ethics grounded in supposed divine revelation or taboo, sanctions that do not appeal to reason.

Hence my concern is with the *irrational* element in belief about sex. Much of what follows is acknowledged superstition; some of it is not. I suggest that the examples cited exhibit a common irrationalism, and that where the irrationalism is with us still perhaps we should get rid of it.

CHAPTER TWO

SUPERSTITION IN PRIMITIVE SOCIETY

In the first communities, superstition was little more than a system of taboo. Later it became necessary to propitiate a whole range of supernatural agencies, capricious spirits infesting the environment and taking a disturbing interest in all man's affairs. In sexual matters people felt especially vulnerable. To transgress taboo or offend the gods could mean sterility or stillbirth; if menstruous women were not treated according to magical prescription then perhaps the sun would no longer shine; if couples copulated at the wrong time then the forthcoming battle would be lost and the crops would not grow.

Plato put into the mouth of Aristophanes a theory as to the origin of men and women.[1] In the first place, we are told, there were three sexes, the third being an hermaphrodite: the male sprang from the sun and the female from the earth, while the sex that was both male and female came from the moon, which partakes of the nature of both sun and earth. Every individual had its back and flanks rounded to form a circle. It had four hands, four legs, and two identical faces upon a circular neck supporting a single head. Each individual carried two organs of generation. When rapid movement was required the creatures turned over and over with a hoop-like progression. Their strength and vigour made them very formidable, and they had immense pride: they attacked the gods, and Homer's story of Ephialtes and Otus attempting to climb up to heaven is related to these beings.

Zeus and his colleagues wanted to teach the creatures a lesson but at the same time were reluctant to destroy the race as they would deprive themselves of the sacrifices and honours due from humanity. At last Zeus had an idea: he decided to cut each of the creatures in two—to weaken them and make them more numerous. Now they walked upright and Zeus threatened that if there was further insolence he would bisect them again, and force them to hop on one leg! To heal the wound Apollo pulled the skin together and tied it in the middle of the belly at an aperture men call the navel.

In the original being the reproductive organs were on the outer side of the body, and the process of procreation was achieved by emission onto the ground, "as is the case with grasshoppers." Now the genitals were moved to the front. Each person having being divided in two, each half yearned for the other, and when two halves met they embraced passionately in the longing to unite. Bisexual reproduction had arrived! The legend is an explanation of both heterosexual and homosexual relations since the two halves that struggle to unite may both be of the same sex.

George Ryley Scott talks of the "androgynous First Principle in creation".[2] When the planets became gods they were seen as androgynous deities, permeated by the essence of the central principle. Even Venus, the symbol of femininity to modern eyes, was viewed as hermaphroditic: Maimonides has been quoted as seeing it affirmed in a book of magic that when a man adored the planet Venus he should wear the embroidered vest of a female; similarly, when a woman adored the planet Mars she should assume the arms and clothing of a man. The ancient temples of Venus contained both consecrated harlots and catamites (boy prostitutes). In the Talmud, the sacred book of the Hebrews, there is a description of an androgynous Adam. Contemporary deities were often regarded as hermaphroditic: thus Phanes, Baal and Phtha.

In ancient Cos, the priests of Hercules felt it necessary to wear female garments when making sacrifices. The Argives practised transvestism at their monthly festivities in honour of the moon. Tacitus records that in ancient Germany male priests were dressed as women, a circumstance paralleled in the Roman rites on the ides of January. Maimonides observed that "the dress excited concupiscence and gave occasion to whoredom."

In Hindu legend, Siva and Parvati originated as the two halves of one androgynous god, Virag; and the great Brahma too was hermaphroditic. Many early statues show the male and female reproductive organs on the one deity. Synesius referred to an Egyptian deity bearing the inscription: "Thou art the father and thou art the mother." And among the Etruscans, the phallus represented both the male and female reproductive powers.

The hermaphroditic gods were thought to reproduce by inserting their own male members into their own female apertures. For this reason many of the phallic gods were represented with elongated sexual organs; in some instances insertion for procreation was thought to be via the mouth, and so the divine phalli had to be at least as long as the trunk.

In many primitive societies the sex act was not associated with conception; and the procreative capacity was thought sometimes to belong solely to women and sometimes solely to men. All human attributes were attributed to individual deities. It would not do, for instance, if women were superior to gods in having, say, breasts—and so a number of the gods were duly assigned a full complement of all the male and female characteristics. An illustration in Gorius shows one divine figure possessing both a penis and female breasts.

At the same time many early communities were fully aware of the dual nature of procreative activity, and the male and female elements—as in Plato's Symposium—were thought to be central features of cosmogony. Many early cave drawings show an awareness of the two components necessary for procreation. Palaeolithic hunters used sympathetic magic not only to ensure capture of wild animals but also to ensure their continued fertility.

Early cave drawings depict female animals attended by rutting males. A clay figure of a mare at Montespan has unnaturally prominent teats:[3] thus the female beasts must be fertile and bear many young to secure the viability of the herd. In 1927, H. Martin discovered a palaeolithic sanctuary at Le Roc-de-Sers (Charente) where fertility magic was assiduously practised. A semicircular platform some 24 feet in diameter was located between two ancient dwelling caves half way up a rock wall. Limestone blocks had been cut in relief and arranged in a semi-circle. Further sculptured stones were found and figures of horses, bison, boars, ibex and human beings were plainly recognizable. Most of the animals are shown with hanging bellies to depict pregnancy, and on one of the blocks a mare is being mounted by a stallion.

Impressive remains of fertility magic have also been found in the Tuc d'Audoubert cave. In a chamber 2,275 feet from the cave mouth a clay relief depicts a pair of bison. The female stands with outstretched neck and raised tail, the clear posture of the cow receiving the bull.

The prehistoric hunters thus aimed, by the use of magic, to bring about couplings among the bison of the region, so that these animals would multiply and form large herds. In Tuc d'Audoubert small clay phallic models were found, clearly employed in magic ritual.

Near Angles-sur-L'Anglin (Vienne), a palaeolithic relief was discovered which depicted three nude female figures: one has the narrow hips of adolescence, another is clearly pregnant. The young girl stands apart, directly above a bison's back. The animal has an upraised tail and is clearly in heat. The stress on the sexual features of the figures show that the composition is not accidental, and illustrate again the early preoccupation with sympathetic magic for pro-creative purposes.

The importance of female fertility in Danubian neolithic life is shown by the exaggerated sex characteristics of the omnipresent idols. Male idols are rarely found. Two idols found in Transylvania, Romania, show the likelihood of fertility rites in the area: the male and female models are carefully contrived and exactly fit into each other *in copula*. Neolithic lake dwellers in Switzerland practised fertility magic similar to that still being carried out in New Guinea.

The idea that symbolic action could stimulate the *actualization* of the required condition is a notion that underlies much primitive ritual: like produces like. The principle also operated when early man detected similarities between the organs of reproduction and other naturally occuring phenomena. . . .

The fig, its shape resembling somewhat that of the female womb, came to be blessed with the same attributes, and to symbolize the womb of the "Mother goddess." Since figs were the *fruit of the tree of life* they came to have a whole range of phallic associations. As the leaves of the tree were used as aprons to cover male and female nudity they came to serve the same purpose with statues in Victorian museums. Phallic statues were carved in many lands from the wood of the fig-tree, and the tree itself was dedicated to Bacchus. Plutarch records that the phalli carried through the streets for the festivals of Priapus were made from the wood of the fig-tree, and a basket of figs featured prominently in the procession.

The oak tree was considered by the ancient Teutons to be male because the acorn in its cupule resembles the *glans penis* with its prepuce. For similar reasons the pomegranate symbolized the female womb in a state of pregnancy, and its immense number of seeds made it suitable as an emblem for a prolific mother goddess. Thus the fruit was common in many ancient temples, and the ancient pagan goddesses, Astarte, Ishtar and Ashtoreth, were frequently adorned with the fruit, as in more modern times was the Virgin Mary.

The phallic associations of the mandrake were due in part to the striking resemblance of its root to the scrotum of man and in part also to its reported aphrodisiacal qualities, to which we find tribute given in the Bible (Genesis 30, 14–16). The lotus, or Egyptian water-lily, was worshipped by the Tartars, the Japanese and the Chinese, as a symbol of the reproductive spirit in nature. Plants analogous to the lotus were employed in many countries to represent the female part in creation, or as symbols of fecundity. To the ancient Hindus the lotus was the emblem of the world, the whole plant indicating the two principles of fecundation. The Mexican fertility goddess, Cinteotl, is sometimes shown bearing in her hand a water plant similar to the lotus.

Fertility rites took on a profound significance for early man and sexual intercourse itself often came to have a mystic significance. In Bali, for instance, with a marriageable age of eighteen for boys and sixteen for girls, Batara Semara is an hermaphrodite deity who made mating a pleasure for women as well as for men: when men and women make love they become one and so imitate the androgynous god.

The sex organs themselves were seen as having magical power, and replicas of phallus and vulva to ward off evil spirits were commonplace in the ancient world.

The majority of objects depicted on urns of the East Teutons have been taken as sexual symbols conceived as a means of defence. In Abyssinia and neighbouring countries the chieftain used to wear a chaplet fitted with a horn representing a phallus; the emperor of Kaffa wore a triple phallic crown; and in the art of Jennissei, male and female sexual organs formed one of the motifs most frequently employed. In 1894, according to one report, phallic figurines were offered for sale by traders in Tiflis. In various parts of Italy a symbol of the vulva was used as defence magic against the threat of the evil eye: the thumb is pressed between the adjoining index finger and the middle finger. The sign is made and shown to anyone with whom one has had a quarrel.

There is a story told in verse (*Priapeia*, Venetiis, 1517; English translation, Cosmopoli, 1890) of a poet affected with phimosis and balanitis, who feared surgery, and therefore visited a statue of Priapus to pray for help: in due course he was cured of the infection. In his supplication to the deity, the poet promised to paint upon a consecrated tablet an exact reproduction in size, shape and colour, of the phallus on the statue of Priapus. Rosenbaum, in advancing this story as an indication of the supposed virtues of phallicism, suggests that it supports his contention that venereal disease led to the introduction of phallic worship.[4]

Priapus attended to afflictions of the male genitals and Isis performed the same duty to women with venereal infection. Rosenbaum again—"the temples of the goddess [Isis] were full of images of parts of the body that had been healed, and

of named organs." Petronius has mentioned worship of the
female buttocks by the ancient Romans, and devil-worship
and witchcraft in the Middle Ages was accompanied by
similar interest in the features of the Roman posterior—a
clear sign of prevalent anal eroticism.

The act of coitus is frequent in ancient art and sculpture.
Phallic objects adorned the huts of villagers and were even
carried around on their persons. In Java an ithyphallic deity
was worshipped by the Ulisiwa tribe, and the god was represented by a man-sized idol. As late as 1917, in one report
(Hartland), phallic idols made of clay and decorated with
feathers were still employed as fetishes by the Bayanzi tribe
on the eastern bank of the Knilm river in the Congo.

The Aztec fertility god, Xopancale, was represented by a
pillar, and in the Mexican town of Panuco the temples and
public squares contained bas-reliefs of men and women
in coitus. At Tlascala, sexual intercourse was venerated
under the phallic symbol representing jointly the male and
female genitals. Grijalva came across representations in
Yucatan of "men committing acts of indescribable beastliness," and Stephens comments with a similar reticence—
"in Yucatan the ornaments upon the external cornice of
several large buildings actually consisted of *membra con-
juncta in coitu*, too plainly sculptured to be misunderstood."

Every New Hebridean village used to have a *Tam-tam*,
consisting of the trunk of a large tree, carved in the image
of a human body and bearing an enormous member. Similarly in Ceylon the Tamil venerates the phallus, and phallic
worship was pronounced in the African state of Dahomey.
Sir Richard Burton records that every street was adorned
with phallic symbols.[5] The Dahomey Priapus was made of
clay and could be any size between a giant and a pigmy,
"crouched upon the ground as if contemplating its own
attributes." A huge penis projected from the middle.

According to one writer, in New Holland, Australia, the
aborigines celebrate their spring festival by shouting and
singing as they dance round a pit which is "so dug and
decorated with bushes as to represent the private parts of a

c

female: as they dance they carry the spear before them to simulate priapus; every gesture is obscene."[6]

Phallic figures and images of the male and female genitalia, some what Scott calls "the most shameless representations," have been found all over the world. Bancroft talks of the "disproportionately large *membrum generationis virile in erectione*" which was the most prominent feature of idols found on Zapetero Island, around Lake Nicaragua, and in Costa Rica. In Java the male and female organs are both subject to adoration, as they were in Tlascala. And one of the companions of Cortez remarked that "in certain countries, and particularly at Panuco, they adore the phallus, and it is preserved in the temples." The Maoris still decorate the rafters of their sacred houses with representations of the male and female genitalia: the reproductive organs are considered to be the ribs of Human House—the human race is carried and supported on the reproductive organs just as a house is supported by the rafters. In Western Africa, phallicism is easily discernible and Seabrook describes phallic statues near a stockade: "at the right of the entrance stood a brave little wooden man with an enormous phallus painted red, and at its left a little wooden woman with an equally emphasized vagina."[7]

One theory of circumcision and other mutilations of the genital organs in early society is that such activities represent a form of sacrifice intended to appease the gods and spirits of the tribe. It has in fact been argued that the blood of circumcision performs the same mystical function as the blood of sacrifice. Transformation of the practice into a religious rite commanded by the god of the Israelites was a clear attempt, on the part of the theologians, to disguise phallicism under another name. Much in the Judeo-Christian tradition smacks of pagan ancestry.

Since the genital organs were so revered in ancient societies, to capture the genitals of one's enemies would represent the ultimate victory. Thus among the people of Mowat it was customary for the victor in battle to wear about him the sexual member of his conquered enemy as a means of increasing virility and strength. A Galla warrior must prove his bravery and skill as a hunter if he wishes to marry. He may be obliged to appear with the testicles of a human enemy as a preliminary to his wedding day. The nomad Danakil, who roamed the dry eastern desert of Ethiopia between the high mountains and the Red Sea, were fanatical collectors of phallic trophies from their fallen enemies. A wife, without such evidence of her husband's valour, would never be received into the circle of other wives. (Compare these practices with 1 Samuel 18, 25, 27 where King Saul asks for a hundred foreskins of Philistines in return for the hand of his daughter Michal—"David brought their foreskins, and they gave them in full tale to the king, that he might be the king's son-in-law.")

In *Marquesan Sexual Behaviour*,[8] Robert C. Suggs describes the behaviour of an old woman to illustrate the magic power thought to attend the genitals: she moves slowly, sweeping with a faggot broom; the rattle of a dried breadfruit leaf shatters her absorption; she rushes to the spot where the leaf will alight; seizing it she quickly thrusts it under her buttocks: The woman was observing an ancient religious practice, honouring the "angry breadfruit-leaf god." The leaf, falling from above her, had removed her supernatural power; so she rendered the leaf profane by placing it beneath her buttocks, close to the contaminating influence of her genitals.

The magical power of the genitals is such that it may be dangerous even to look at them. In Tanna and Malekula, for instance, reported by Crawley,[9] the closest secrecy was adopted with regard to the penis, not from a sense of decency, but to avoid *narak*: the sight of the penis of another man could have untold magical consequences. The organ was therefore wrapped round with many yards of calico, wound and folded until a bundle two feet long is formed. Not surprisingly to *touch* the sex organs illicitly may also be frought with great dangers: thus during the shaving or depilation of the male sex organs of the Pamil coolies of Malabar, it was customary for the barber to insert the penis into a bamboo tube, which he holds and uses as a handle; he is not allowed to touch the venerated organ.

Nor is it safe, at all times, to use the organs in sexual intercourse. A complicated framework of prohibition on carnal
relations in primitive society grew up. Abstinence from sex
was mandatory in many circumstances. Intending priests
were obliged to refrain from sexual activity; only by remaining "pure" could they expect to employ the magic for the
good of the tribe. Thus the "ordeal of fire" in various
tribes of Africa is preceded by a period of restraint from
sexual activity. The candidate priest who is being tested
steps into a circle of fire, which is fed until the flames are
higher than the man's head: if he has abstained from sex
during the prescribed period he emerges unscathed, and if
he cannot survive the ordeal then clearly he is not pure. This
attitude is common among primitive people, that purification by sexual restraint gives the priest greater persuasive
power with the ever-present spirits. (Without further comment the link between these superstitious attitudes and the
celibate obligations in the Roman Catholic priesthood should
be obvious.)

Robert Suggs, writing of the Marquesans, notes a number
of instances where abstinence from sexual intercourse is
demanded of sacred personages. The *tuhuka o'oko* was a
bard of the tribe, with revered functions as official historian and genealogist. His duties included reciting genealo-
gies, chants and legends in appropriate ceremonies throughout the course of the year. Individuals selected to fill the post
were not allowed to use cosmetics linked with sex, and during periods of instruction, usually lasting a month, they were
obliged to abstain from sexual activity. Below the specialist
tuhuka o'oko were a mass of native priests of inferior status,
specializing in divination and prophecy, magic, medicine,
and various other pursuits. These individuals were expected
to exercise sexual abstinence during the period of their
religious functions.

The Tahitians held that if a man abstained from sexual
intercourse for some months before his death, his lot was
improved in the hereafter. Abstinence has also been a widespread requirement for mourning purposes. In mourning a
New Caledonian chief, the required sexual abstinence was

expected to last up to one month. In Sierra Leone sexual intercourse is forbidden for ten days in mourning a commoner, and thirty days for a person of importance; in Whydah, sexual intercourse was forbidden for a whole year of mourning.

A widower of the Stlatlum tribe in British Columbia was also required to forego sexual relations for a year. In such circumstances, he would exile himself in the forest and seek "mystery powers." Similar prohibitions applied in many ancient societies: Hindus abstained for ten days of mourning; in Egypt for seventy-two days of mourning for a king. Perhaps the ancient Chinese hold the record—sexual abstinence for the full three years of the mourning period.

Women in New Caledonia were forbidden sexual intercourse for a specific time before and after performing their tasks. Similarly the Thompson River women of British Columbia were required to live chastely while digging and cooking the sunflower root. Conjugal abstinence was observed in ancient Mexico—for five days before the feast to the divinity Mixcoatl, the god of the tornado, and for four days before that to Tlaloc, the god of rain. A similar rule operated in Peru in preparing for the annual sun festival of Raymi.

Military expeditions were likely to be threatened by sexual intercourse. The Indians in British Columbia were obliged to abstain from sexual activity for three or four weeks before setting out on a campaign. Similarly, the Shushwap Indian loses the supernatural power he acquires with his guardian spirit if he sees a woman when he is on his way to war. One writer, quoted by Crawley, remarked that "after having had sexual intercourse men as well as women become . . . weak, incapable of gaining supernatural powers." Further—"the faculties cannot be regained by subsequent fasting and abstinence." The North American Indians generally used not to cohabit with women while they were engaged in war.

The hunters among the Tinnehs in British Columbia tried to achieve good luck by severe washings, fasting, and not touching a woman for two or three months. The Western Tinneh felt it necessary to leave his marriage bed for ten days before going on a marten-hunt, for a month in the case of a bear-hunt. Nor must his wife approach or step over the snare, for if she did all further efforts to catch the animal would be futile. The Dakota purifies himself by sexual abstinence, and if his weapons are touched by a woman they will at once be rendered useless. In similar spirit, the Creek Indians reckoned that sexual intercourse made them unfit as warriors, and the Sia of New Mexico used to abstain for four days before going hunting. According to the Huichols of Mexico a deer would never enter a snare set by a man who is in love.

Before a war the South African Bantus performed ceremonies for sexual purification, and a native African has been quoted as saying of the Zulu warriors—"no one among them is able to associate with his wife; they abstain excessively; for if a man, when the army is going out . . . associate with his wife, he kills himself, making his own eyes dark." The women were not allowed to approach the army as it prepared for battle. An exception to the rule was permitted to *old* women since they "have become men."

The Wagiriami of British East Africa believed that if men were to sleep with their wives during wartime they would be unable to kill any of their enemies and that if they themselves received a trifling wound it would prove fatal.

In *Sex Life and Sex Ethics*[10] René Guyon quotes a number of prohibitions on sexual activity in primitive society, mostly taken from Frazer's *Golden Bough:*

> When a chief priest of the Congo travelled to mete out justice married persons must refrain from sexual intercourse; otherwise the priest would meet with disaster.

> In Assam a chief had to abstain from sexual relations on the day before a public observance of taboo; otherwise the ceremony would fail in its purpose.

> Among the Ba-Pedis and the Ba-Tongas of South Africa, sexual abstinence was demanded not only of warriors on a military task, but of the folk who remained behind in the village.

Among the Burmese Kochins a woman who prepares yeast for making beer must abstain from sex; otherwise the beer would be bitter.

The gathering of the sacred cactus by the Huichol Indians in Mexico could be guaranteed successful only if the people back home refrained from sexual indulgence while the cactus was being gathered.

In Sarawak, a wife's infidelity was thought likely to interfere with her absent husband's search for camphor.

In connection with general fertility of crop and beast the opposite principle has frequently been enjoined. Frazer tells us that for four days before committing the seed to the earth the Pipiles of Central America kept apart from their wives "in order that on the night before planting they might indulge their passions to the fullest extent."[11] Persons were even appointed to copulate at the very moment when the first seeds were deposited on the ground. It was not lawful to sow the seed unless accompanied by suitable human couplings.

In some parts of Java, at the time when the bloom would soon be on the rice, the husbandman and his wife used to visit their fields by night and there indulge in sexual relations for the purpose of promoting the growth of the crop. The Baganda of Central Africa often cast out a barren wife, since she was supposed to prevent her husband's garden from bearing fruit. By contrast, parents of twins are seen to be possessed of unusual procreative power, and efforts were made, by dint of magical ritual, to transfer their fruitfulness to the earth: the mother lies down on her back in the grass near her house and places a flower of the plantain between her legs; then her husband knocks the flower away with his penis, so ensuring that the crops will be fertile.

In various islands between New Guinea and the northern part of Australia the population regards the sun as the male principle by whom the earth, the female principle, is fertilized. They call the sun, appropriately enough, Upu-lera or

Mr Sun, and represent him in the sacred fig-tree. Under the tree is a stone sacrificial table. On it, until quite recently, the heads of slain enemies were placed. Once a year, at the start of the rainy season, Mr Sun comes down into the holy fig-tree to fertilize the earth, and to aid his descent a ladder with seven rungs is placed at his disposal. On this sacred occasion vast numbers of pigs and dogs are sacrificed, and men and women indulge in an orgy. The object of the procedure is to ensure a general fruitfulness, to procure rain, abundance of food and drink, plenty of cattle and children.

In the Babar Islands a special flag is hoisted at the festival as a symbol of the creative power of the sun. The flag is of white cotton, about nine feet high, and carries the figure of a man in what Frazer terms "an appropriate attitude." The accompanying orgies are deliberately and solemnly organized as crucial to the fertility of the earth and the consequent welfare of human society.

In some parts of Amboyna, when the look of the clove plantation suggests that the crop is likely to be poor, the men go naked to the plantations at night and there proceed to ejaculate upon the trees to fertilize them. At the same time they call out for "More cloves!" In the Ukraine on St George's Day the priest used to go out to the fields of the village, where the crops are beginning to show green above the ground, to bless them. After that the young married people of the village roll over together over the sown ground.

Sometimes sexual abstinence, not indulgence, was the rule to promote bountiful crops. The Indians of Nicaragua used to live chastely from the moment they sowed the maize until the time that it was reaped. Before sowing the maize the Ketchi Indians used to sleep away from their wives, and eat no fish for five days! The period of abstinence for the Lanquineros and Cajaboneros extended to thirteen days. Among the Germans of Transylvania it was a rule that no man should sleep with his wife during the whole time that he is occupied with sowing the fields. Similarly, at old Kalotaszeg in Hungary: people there used to think that if the custom were not observed the crops would be mildewed. A Central Australian headman of the Kaitish tribe was obliged to refrain from carnal pleasures during the magical ceremonies to make the grass grow. In some of the Melanesian islands, the men were expected not to approach their wives while the yam vines were being trained.

The varying primitive attitudes to sexual intercourse have been parallelled by similarly diverse beliefs about the associated human states—such as loss of virginity, the state of marriage, childbirth, etc. Important chiefs in the Congo used to keep in their service a virgin to care for the arrows, shields, rugs and other war equipment. It was thought that the girl's virginity lent the weapons some extraordinary virtue and power. If the girl custodian is remiss enough to lose her virginity, the articles are destroyed as dangerous to those who might use them.

Unless medicine-women of certain Guarani tribes in Paraguay remained chaste they were considered to have lost their effectiveness. And magical power was ascribed to the virgin sun-brides of Peru who received a message from Prince Uiraccocha, after his great victory over the Chancas, announcing the triumph "which had been granted in return for their prayers and *merits*." Similarly with the Roman Vestal virgins, their "purity" ensured their supernatural power. Once, when the sacred fire went out and the responsible Vestal was suspected of unchastity rather than carelessness, she tore off a piece of her linen garment and threw it upon the altar: a great flame shot out from the ashes in proof of her innocence.

In many early communities virgin girls had to be deflowered before they could be regarded as acceptable marriage partners. The blood following the rupture of a hymen was held in awe as possessing fearsome magical properties. In consequence, deflowering had to be done by some person immune to the powerful magic. Thus various types of holy men, such as priests, kings and chiefs, enjoyed certain privileges in early society: they were credited with the power to deflower a virgin with impunity. Westermarck has shown in *The History of Human Marriage* that among the Sinhalese, a father could claim the right of deflowering his own daughter before marriage, asserting a right "to the first-fruit of the tree he had planted." In other instances, says Westermarck, defloration was carried out by a member of some alien tribe who, being considered a sort of semi-supernatural being, was not only immune from the effects of contact with the blood but could also confer beneficial effects upon the fortunate girl in question.

In some instances civil servants were employed for the task. A passage has been quoted from Gemelli Cancri, communicated by Jager to the Berlin Anthropological Society, on practices among the Bisayos of the Philippine Islands—"There is no known experience of a custom so barbarous as that which had been there established of having public officials, and even paid very dearly, to take the virginity of young girls, the same being considered to be an obstacle to the pleasures of the husband."

The value placed by certain folk in our society on virginity at the time of marriage would have been viewed as a strange eccentricity by many earlier peoples. Some early men were even keen that their brides should already be mothers, to have clear demonstration of that much vaunted fertility. Among most tribes of Kamchatka a girl was disgraced if she entered marriage as a virgin: concientious mothers widened the vagina of their daughters with their fingers from early youth. In Northern Australia defloration is carried out with a stick, while the aborigines of New South Wales used to employ a piece of flint for the same purpose. In Azimbaland (Central Africa) a horn or horn-stick was driven into the vagina of young girls; on the Sawu Islands a cork was preferred. In Samoa defloration used formerly to be carried out in public, the girl lying on a special mat and the hymen being pierced with a small stick.

In some societies where defloration has been associated with the supernatural, the phallus of an idol is used to rupture the virgin hymen. The girls of the Canaries used to sit over the phallus of a stone idol for this purpose.

Puberty, particularly female puberty with the onset of menstrual bleeding, was a particularly dangerous time for the primitive community. Some societies thought that the first menstruation was caused by the presence of a spirit inside the girl's body: as with medieval witches, the accepted practice was to beat the person's body until the demon was forced to flee. Thus the widespread practice of scourging of virgins. Amongst the Ungonimos, a tribe that used to live on the banks of the Amazon, a girl at puberty was taken out of a place of concealment, bound naked to a tree, and beaten with scourges of knotted grass into which stones have been plaited. At the same time a witch-doctor conjured the evil spirit possessing her to depart forthwith. Scourging girls in such a fashion used to be practised in a number of tribes, for example in the communities of Afar and Somaliland in North East Africa. When a Christian marriage was celebrated in Mossul old women sat at the bride's feet and pricked them with needles. Among the Hausan Arabs on the upper reaches of the Nile and with some Hindu tribes the bridegroom was scourged. In Madagascar he was forced to ward off spears hurled at him. In Polynesia it used to be customary to beat newly-wed couples. In France it was the custom to hit the bridal pair on the head during the wedding service. And in the Upper Palatinate the marriage announcer struck the bride betweeen the shoulders with the blade of a sword, and did the same when she approached the altar.

The time of puberty, especially for girls, has often been seen as a hazardous period in their lives. In many parts of the world, girls at puberty were (a) not allowed to touch the ground, and (b) not allowed to see the sun. Thus amongst the negroes of Loango girls at puberty were confined in special huts, and they were not permitted to touch the ground with any part of their bare body. Among the Zulus, when a girl noticed her first menstruation, she must run to hide herself so as not to be seen by men. If the sun were to shine on her at such a time she would instantly shrivel up into a withered skeleton, and so she carefully covered her head with a blanket. After dark she was allowed to return home and seclusion in a hut followed. With the Awa-nkonde, a tribe that used to live at the northern end of Lake Nyassa, it used to be a rule that after her first menstruation a girl must be kept apart in a darkened house, which was called "the house of the Awusungu," i.e. "of maidens who have no hearts."

In New Ireland girls used to be kept in small cages for four or five years (!), in the dark and not allowed to set foot on the ground. Frazer, from whom these examples are taken, quotes an eye-witness:

> . . . then the girls peeped out at us, and, when told to do so, they held out their hands for the beads. I, however, purposely sat at some distance away and merely held out the beads to them, as I wished to draw them quite outside, that I might inspect the inside of the cages . . . these girls were not allowed to put their feet on the ground all the time they were confined in these places . . . the old lady had to go outside and collect a lot of pieces of wood and bamboo, which she placed on the ground, and then going to one of the girls, she helped her down and held her hand as she stepped from one piece of wood to another. . . . The girls are never allowed to come out except once a day to bathe . . . One of them was about fourteen or fifteen years old, and the chief told us that she had been there for four or five years, but would soon be taken out now.

Similarly, in Kabadi, a district of British New Guinea, it was the custom to keep the daughters of chiefs, when they were about twelve or thirteen years of age, indoors for two or three years, never allowed to descend from the house; and the house is shaded so that the sun cannot shine on them. The Ot Danoms of Borneo used to shut up girls of eight or ten years in a little room or cell. The girl was in almost total darkness and could not leave the house on any pretext whatever, not even for what Frazer terms "the most necessary purposes." None of her family might see her all the time she was locked away, but she was allocated a slave girl to feed her. In some cases the forced imprisonment could last for as long as seven years. Not surprisingly, the bodily growth of such a girl was stunted, and when brought out, on attaining womanhood, her complexion was pale and waxlike. The woman is shown the sun, the earth, the trees, as if she were newly born. It was then the custom to make a great feast, to kill a slave, and to smear the young woman with his blood.

In Ceram girls were shut up in a dark hut. In Yap, one of the Caroline Islands, if a girl began her first menstruation on a public road, she could not sit down but was obliged to beg for a coconut shell to put under her. She too had then to be confined in a small hut for several days, and afterwards for a hundred days in one of the special buildings reserved for the use of menstruous women.

On some islands of the Torres Straits special arrangements were made when the first signs of puberty appeared in a girl. A circle of bushes was arranged in a dark corner of the house and the girl was decked out in shoulder-belts, armlets, leglets and anklets, wearing a chaplet on her head, and shell ornaments in her ears, on her chest, and on her back. Decorated in such a fashion she used to squat in the midst of the bushes with only her head visible. In this state of seclusion she was obliged to remain for three months. Sometimes, at night, she was allowed out briefly, to permit the bushes to be changed. During this time the sun was not to shine on her, she could not feed herself or handle food, she could not eat turtle or turtle-eggs during the turtle breeding season, and no man could come into the house while her seclusion lasted: if her father entered the house at this time he would be sure to have bad luck in his fishing and would probably have an accident in his canoe the next time he used it.

When the three months was over, she was carried down to a fresh-water creek in such a fashion that her feet did not touch the ground. She was then stripped of all her ornaments and immersed in the water, after which she was forced to squat on a heap of grass. An attendant caught a small crab, tore off its claws, and roasted them at a fire. The girl is then fed, freshly decorated, and walked back to the village. Great revelries then ensue.

Among the Aht or Nootka Indians of Vancouver Island girls at puberty used to be surrounded by heaps of mats so that they could see neither the sun nor any fire. For several days they were given water but no food, and the longer the girl remained in this predicament the greater honour it was to her parents. If it was found out that she had seen fire or the sun during this period then she was disgraced for life. For all the days of seclusion the girl was not permitted to stand or lie down, but was compelled to squat in a sitting position. Further, she might not touch her hair with her hands but was allowed a comb or a piece of bone for the purpose. Nor was she allowed to scratch her body, for every scratch, however gentle, would leave a scar. For eight months after reaching maturity, she could not eat any fresh food, particularly salmon, and she had to eat on her own during this period.

Amongst the Tsetsaut tribe of British Columbia a girl at puberty wore a large hat so that she could not see the sun, mittens to prevent her naked hands from contaminating other objects, and she carried the tooth of an animal in her mouth to prevent her own teeth from becoming hollow. For a year she might not see blood unless her face was blackened; otherwise she would grow blind. In other tribes of British Columbia, menstruous girls were forced to remain for several days in a special room, bound to remain motionless in a sitting posture. Early in the morning a girl was allowed a little food and drink, her food being put in at a little window. Again she wore a hat with long flaps, that her gaze might not pollute the sky; it was also thought that her look would bring bad fortune to hunters, fishers and gamblers, turn things to stone, and accomplish many other unwelcome things. At the end of her confinement her clothes were immediately burnt, a feast was held, and a slit cut in her underlip, a piece of wood or shell inserted to keep the aperture open. The Guaranis of Southern Brazil used to sew up their girls at puberty in a small hammock, leaving only a small opening in it for them to breathe. Shrouded in such a fashion like a corpse a girl was kept for the duration of the first menstruation, after which an attendant cut her hair and urged her to abstain from eating flesh of any sort until her hair had grown to cover her ears. Some Bolivian tribes used to keep their girls in a similar hammock, but hoisted up to the roof, where the poor creatures were obliged to remain for a month; as a concession the hammock was lowered for a

second month of imprisonment; and in the third month old
women with sticks used to rush into the room shouting that
they were hunting the snake that had wounded the girl.
There is a famous quote in Pliny—

It will not be easy to find anything with more miraculous
effect than the menstrual blood of women. If they are in
this condition and come in contact with new wine it turns
sour, at their touch the fruits of the field become unfruitful, grafts and cuttings wither away, seeds in the garden
are parched and fruit falls from the tree under which a
woman with her periods has sat. Should they look into a
mirror its brilliance is blurred, the blade of an iron knife is
blunted. Ivory loses its lustre, even bronze and iron rust
and give forth an evil odour. Dogs which lap up menstrual
blood go mad and their bite works as a poison for which
there is no cure.

Frazer tells of an Australian "black-fellow" who discovered
that his wife had lain on his blanket during her menstruation: he killed her and died of terror himself within a fortnight. Menstruous women are therefore forbidden to touch
anything that a man uses. Among certain American tribes,
girls were segregated from all company as soon as there was
the slightest sign of menstruation. They were not allowed to
touch venison lest the hunters have increased difficulty in
killing the members of a species so slighted. Menstruous
women were only allowed dried fish and cold water. And as
the very sight of her was dangerous to society the woman
with a period was obliged to move among her people with a
massive bonnet on her head to hide her from view.

Marquesan women, when menstruating, were not allowed
to step over any useful object or structures, or to pass over
the heads of individuals. Thus a woman in that condition
could not sit on a man's saddle, ride in a canoe, or sit on a
house porch if a child were beneath it. If a woman were remiss enough to behave in such a fashion the contamination
could only be removed by killing the woman, destroying the
object, or performing the *ha'a tahe tahe* rite. In this rite, the

woman and the offended party, both nude, entered a stream. The woman stood upstream and splashed the offended party with water that had come into contact with her genitals. In such a fashion could the contamination of the menstrual state be removed.

It is surprising also to see how the primitive superstitions survived in more modern times. Not long ago it was widely believed in Europe that a man who is stained with menstrual blood compels a reluctant maiden to give herself to him. The Archives of the Naples Inquisition for the year 1603 have recorded the case of the Prince of Venosa who was given menstrual blood to drink by one of his mistresses. When the Prince died four *dottori fisici* ascribed his fatal disease to the drinking of blood. A criminal case occurring in 1923 in the Vienna suburb of Simmering has established the modern survival of belief in blood as a love philtre.

As with menstruation so with childbirth. The blood accompanying the new-born infant was thought, as with the menstrual discharge, to possess magic power. The modern practice of "churching" women is clearly derived from the early superstitions about the "impurity" of a woman at and immediately after childbirth.

The danger thought to attend women at the time of their sexual and procreative crises inevitably led to their segregation from menfolk in the community. In the Caroline Islands men used not to eat with their wives during pregnancy, and in Fiji a pregnant woman could not wait upon her husband. On the island of Kisar pregnant women used to take a knife with them when they left the house to frighten away the evil spirits. Among the Basutos pregnant women were thought to be particularly susceptible to witchcraft and wore skin aprons to protect themselves. In a number of Brazilian tribes it was customary for women to remain separate from their husbands throughout the whole period of pregnancy. And in Costa Rica a woman pregnant for the first time was thought to infect the whole neighbourhood: all deaths were blamed on her and her husband was forced to pay damages. A Damara man believed he would be enfeebled if he saw a pregnant woman.

In some primitive communities a woman who had had a miscarriage was customarily fed at the end of a stick, for a period of three weeks or longer. If a woman, fearing the consequences of exposure, *concealed* the aborted foetus then many grave consequences might ensue. Fielding[12] quotes a medicine-man of the Ba-Pedi tribe:

> When a woman has had a miscarriage, when she has allowed her blood to flow, and has hidden the child, it is enough to cause the burning winds to blow and to parch the country with heat. The rain no longer falls, for the country is no longer in order. When the rain approaches the place where the blood is, it will not dare come further. ... That woman has committed a great fault. She has spoiled the country of the chief, for she has hidden her blood which had not yet been well congealed to fashion a man. That blood is taboo.

The woman is forced to reveal where she hid the foetus: the hole is then sprinkled with special root preparations, and the woman herself must wash every day with the medicine. Only by such means can continued drought be averted.

In the Marquesas Islands all women were prohibited from using canoes, and the breaking of the rule was punishable by death. The Kaffirs would not let women touch their cattle, and among the Dakotas women were prohibited from touching anything that related to the sphere of male activity. In the Marquesas, if a woman happened to sit upon the stool of a man by accident, the stool could never be used again and the woman was put to death. In the same region the houses of important men were not accessible to their wives who were obliged to live in adjoining huts. In Tahiti and the Society Islands generally a woman was not allowed to visit those places frequented by men, and the head of a father and husband was "sacred" from the touch of a woman. Nor might a wife or daughter touch an article that had been in contact with the tabooed heads. Similarly, no woman was allowed to enter the house of a Maori chief, and it was not thought well for a Fijian husband to spend much time with his wife. In

D

New Caledonia men took care not to be seen often in the society of the opposite sex.

In Cambodia a wife was not allowed to use the pillow or mattress of her husband, because—in the words of one writer—"she would hurt his happiness thereby." In Siam it was thought unlucky to pass under a woman's clothes hung out to dry. Among the Karens of Burma men used to take care to avoid going into a house within which there were women present, and throughout Burma it was considered inappropriate to have a woman "above" one, which is why, according to Bastian, houses in Burma were never built with more than one storey. If a Bengalese man was detected by a woman sitting on her cot, and she complained, he would pay her a fowl as a fine, which she then returned; if on the other hand a man discovered a woman sitting on his cot, he would kill a fowl which she produced, and sprinkle the blood on the cot to purify it, after which the woman was pardoned.

Zulus traditionally treated their wives with a haughty contempt, and men and women were rarely seen together. If a woman stepped over the legs of a sleeping Bantu man, it was thought he would never walk again. And amongst the Barea of East Africa man and wife did not share a bed since it was thought that the woman's breath would make a man weak. Kaffa wives were kept in one room of the house; if they infringed the man's quarters, the rest of the building, a penalty of three years' imprisonment was applied.

It was also a widespread custom for women to be excluded from religious activity, as they are today in connection with the various Christian priesthoods. Thus in the Sandwich Islands women were never allowed to share in festivals or worship, and their touch was thought to pollute offerings to the gods. In the Marquesas the *hoolah-hoolah* ground, where festivals are held, was taboo to women, who were killed if they entered it or even if their feet touched the shadow of its trees.

Primitive man was always worried that undue contact with his wife would make him weak. Hence the maxim in Hesiod that a man should not wash in water used by his wife, and in Homer, Odysseus fears that he might be "unmanned" and therefore susceptible to Circe's influence if he ascended her couch. Crawley quotes a Khyoungthas legend of a man who reduced a king and his followers to a condition of feebleness by persuading them to dress up as women and perform female duties: when they had been thus rendered effeminate they could no longer fight and were defeated without a blow.

The Dyaks of North-West Borneo would not let young men eat venison, which is the peculiar food of women and old men, since it would render the men timid as deer. During his period of initiation a medicine-man in Central Australia had to sleep with a fire between him and his wife, for if he did not do so his power would disappear for ever. In South Africa a man was not supposed to touch his wife in bed with his right hand, lest he lose all his strength and be slain in war.

Sometimes the contempt for what is imagined to be innate female timidity has led to barbaric customs. Among the Gallas, for example, it used to be customary to amputate the mammae of boys soon after birth, since the nipples symbolize femininity and no man could be brave who possessed them. In many societies it was the rule that impotent and weak men were downgraded to the lower status of women, forced to wear their clothes and perform the most menial of tasks. Such men existed in, for example, many of the tribes of California, and were called *i-wa-musp*, man-woman.

But while women were regarded as timid creatures and the natural inferiors of men, it was also thought that they possessed strange magical powers. In the Arunta, women were supposed to be able to work magic in connection with a man's sex organs, making him impotent, sterile, etc: much in the way that medieval witches were thought to operate.

An Arunta woman would aim at harming a man's sex organs by first procuring the spear-like seed of a long grass (*Inturkirra*), then, after singing a chant over it, throwing it in the direction of the man she wished to injure. At once, so we are told, his genitals would swell painfully. Or a woman might charm a handful of dust, sprinkling the dust over a spot were the man is likely to urinate. If he should do so at this spot he would experience a scalding sensation in the urethra. Women were also thought able to produce disease in men by "singing over," i.e. charming, one of their own fingers which is then inserted into the vagina. The man who next has sexual intercourse with such a woman would inevitably become diseased and might lose his genitals altogether. Not surprisingly, syphilitic disease among the Arunta was frequently attributed to this form of magic.

Despite woman's low status in primitive society she was nevertheless assigned various magical functions. In some societies women were given the task of planting new seedlings since they give birth to children and would thus convey some of their fruitfulness to the earth. In Malinowski's writings about the Trobrianders[13] we find a division of magical activity on a basis of sex, the sexes being responsible for the following.

Male	Female	Mixed
Public garden magic	Rites of first pregnancy	Beauty magic
Fishing	Skirt making	Love magic
Hunting	Prevention of dangers at	Private garden magic
Canoe building	birth	
Magic of *kula*	Toothache	
Weather (sun and rain)	Elephantiasis	
Wind	Affections of the genitals with discharge	
War magic	Abortion	
Safety at sea	Female witchcraft	
Wood carving		
Sorcery		

The different magical forces thought to reside variously in men and women made it inevitable that the sexes should be separated in many everyday activities in the village. Sometimes, for example, women were not allowed to eat tiger's flesh with the men lest it make them too strong-minded. In Halmahera a pregnant woman never ate food left by her husband for fear that it would give her a difficult labour. It was thought in Hannover-Wendland and the Altmark that if a boy and girl were baptized in the same water the boy would become a woman-hunter, the girl would grow a beard. Similarly, a girl in Neumark baptized in water used for a boy would grow a moustache; in Mecklenburg a boy baptized in water used for a girl was expected to be beardless as a man. It is recorded that Hessian lads used to think they could avoid conscription by carrying a baby-girl's cap in their pocket.

In many primitive societies it was thought obligatory that the sexes be kept apart at all times other than sexual intercourse. A consequence of such attitudes has been the growth of cultural diversity between men and women living in close proximity to each other. In some instances separate language details have been recorded in the verbal usage of men and women, different modes of expression being thought appropriate for the two sexes. Thus the island Caribs used to have two distinct vocabularies, one used by men and by women when speaking to men, and the other used by women when speaking to each other, and by men when repeating some saying of the women. Councils of war were held in a secret dialect or jargon, into which the women were never initiated. In the language of the Abipones some words varied according to which sex was using them, and among the Arawak, men and women had different words even for common objects. Similarly, the Karaya women had a special dialect thought to be an older form of the tribal speech, retained solely by the women and not understood by the men.

Such speech variations on a sex basis can be found in most parts of the world. Thus the Eskimo women of the Mackenzie Delta had expressions, words and terminations which the men do not use, and the women of Greenland were said to have a particular pronunciation peculiar to themselves, and different to that of the men. The Fijian term for a newly circumcised boy is *teve*, which may not be uttered when women are present, in which case the word *kula* is used, and there are many words in the language which are taboo in female society (compare this superstition with the habit in modern society of men using language in male company that they would not wish their wives to hear).

In Japan, female writing had a quite different syntax and many peculiar idioms: and the old Japanese alphabet possessed two sets of characters, *katakana* for the use of men and *hiragana* for the use of women. A Hindu wife was never allowed to mention the name of her husband, and had to refer to him obliquely as "the master" or "the man of the house." If a husband's name appeared in his wife's dreams this would surely lead to a speedy death. Among the Todas there was reluctance to mention the names of women at all: instead it was necessary to use a phrase such as "the wife of so-and-so." In the Pelew Islands, men were not allowed to speak openly of women if they were married, nor to utter their names. Similarly, a Basuto woman was not allowed to speak her husband's name, and this sometimes led to peculiar difficulties: if her husband happened to be called *Lerotholi* (drop), for example, the wife might not say *lerotholi la metsi* (a drop of water), but must use a circumlocution such as *malhlatsa a pula* (a vomiting of rain). Women among the Barea and the Kaffirs were likewise not allowed to speak their husband's names in any circumstances. These examples, which could be extended, illustrate in part the power thought to reside in certain sounds—analogous to the modern fear of *four-letter words*—and in part the consequence of segregating the sexes. The development of private languages according to sex has been noted in modern times. Westermarck has drawn attention to the situation that existed among the Berbers of the Great Atlas, where the women used the old Berber numerals and the men invariably used the Arabic loan-words: the segregation of women was such that they did not have access to numeric innovation.

The marriage ceremony was another event bringing dread to the heart of primitive man. Among the ancient Hindus, for example, it was essential that omens be used in the choice of a suitable marriage-day. Before two children were even betrothed it was thought essential to cast a precise horoscope. First marriages were solemnized only in the spring. When a young man was on his way to ask the girl's parents for her hand in marriage he would watch out for animals carefully—cats, foxes, jackals and snakes were bad omens; mongooses good ones.

In South Germany the garments of the bridal pair had to

be blessed, and the priest prayed hopefully—"may every on-set of evil spirits be brought to nought." The marriage bed was blessed in Upper Bavaria. In old French *Romans d'aven-ture* the bridal pair were often blessed as they lay in bed. The dangers attending defloration could only be countered in some societies by getting the priest, suitably reinforced by appropriate magic, to perform the first act of sexual intercourse on the new bride.

New brides in old China were thought likely to be attacked by evil spirits, causing them to be ill: hence the figure of a "great magician" (a Taoist priest), brandishing a sword, was painted on the sedan-chair used on the wedding-day. The sedan-chair in which the Manchu bride went to the house of the bridegroom had to be disinfected with incense to drive away evil spirits, and in it was placed a calendar containing the names of idols who control the spirits of evil. In Russia, all doors, windows, and even the chimneys, used to be closed at a wedding to stop malicious witches flying in and hunting the bride and bridegroom. The Chuvashes used to honour their wizards (*iemzyas*) and always invited them to weddings, for fear that an offended *iemzya* might kill the bride and bridegroom.

The Manus people, described by the American anthropologist Margaret Mead,[14] believed that the spirits of their recently dead ancestors watched their behaviour, particularly their sexual lives, with great concern, visiting sickness and misfortune on violators of the sexual code. In some instances the spirits might even attempt carnal relations with human women. The Tikopia, according to Firth,[15] thought dream experiences of a sexual type were held to be inspired by malignant demons who assumed the form of a person of the opposite sex, even of a near relative, and invited the dreamer to copulate: on awakening the deed took place. Similarly in some tribes it was thought that the menstrual flow was caused by the bite of a supernatural animal or by congress with an evil spirit. Thus certain Australian tribes used to believe that menstruation came from dreaming that a bandicoot had scratched the genitals. In New Britain such ideas found an artistic expression: one illustration shows a bird drawing something from out of a woman's vagina. A carving on a piece of wood from New Guinea shows one crocodile gripping the head of a woman while a second crocodile is thrusting its snout into the woman's genitals. A similar plank carving shows a snake crawling from a woman's vagina. In Portugal it was believed that during menstruation women were likely to be bitten by lizards: to guard against this risk, drawers were worn. And in New Guinea women were not permitted to eat eels because a god once took the form of an eel to approach a woman while she was bathing. In some cases a belief in the sexual activities of spirits is extended to the point when physical paternity is denied, and the siring of children is achieved by supernatural agencies. The Trobrianders studied by Malinowski believed that the whole process of generation lies between the spirit world and the female organism.

To understand the Trobriander concept of birth we have to start with death. At the moment of death the spirit journeys to Tuma, the Island of the Dead, where a generally blissful existence is led. After a while, however, the spirit feels he would like to return to earth again, and so he leaps back in age and becomes a tiny pre-born infant. This creature then strives to find its way into the womb of a woman who belongs to the same clan and sub-clan as the spirit child itself. Thus every child born in the world has first come into existence in Tuma through the metamorphosis of a spirit. The Trobrianders also have an explanation of how the new spirit child manages to enter the body of the appropriate woman. Malinowski quotes a certain Tomwaya Lakwabulo—

A child floats on a drift log. A spirit sees it is good-look- ing. She takes it. She is the spirit of the mother or of the father of the pregnant woman (*nasusuma*). Then she puts it on the head, in the hair, of the pregnant woman, who suffers headache, vomits, and has an ache in the belly. Then the child comes down into the belly, and she is really pregnant. She says: "Already it (the child) has found me; already they (the spirits) have brought me the child."

Some natives believed that the older spirits carried the baby in a plaited coconut basket or wooden dish, or else simply in their arms. The controlling spirit usually appears in a dream to the woman about to be pregnant, and often a woman will tell her husband who it was that brought the baby to her. Thus, in the Malinowski account, the chief of Omarakana believed it was Bugwabwaga, one of his predecessors in office, who gave him to his mother. Similarly Tokulubakiki was a gift to his mother from her mother's brother. Usually it was some maternal relative of the prospective mother who brought the gift of a child.

We have seen that the spirit-child is laid by the bringer on the mother's head: blood from her body rushes there, and on this tide of blood the baby gradually descends until it settles in the womb. The blood helps to build the body of the, child, which is why, when a woman becomes pregnant, she no longer menstruates.

Associated with the idea of insertion *per vaginam* is the ready awareness that virgins do not conceive—"When the orifice is wide open, the spirits are aware, they give the child." Thus the vagina needs to be open, but the way can be cleared by means other than sexual intercourse. In Trobriander belief, once a girl's *kalapatu* (tightness) has been removed she can conceive, and there is no need for a man and a woman to come together in order to produce a child.

The Trobriander belief can be compared with that of the Australian Aborigines who believed that a woman becomes pregnant when a spirit enters her body. However, anthropologists have varied in their assessment of Aboriginal sex knowledge.[16] In such a primitive society, the link between coitus and conception is not obvious. It is known of course that many girls who have sexual relations do not in fact conceive: the causal situation is difficult to analyse. As Abbie notes, the girl is often protected by the relative sterility of adolescence, and so the first child is not born until four or five years after the first sexual experience. Sometimes Aboriginal women would be lent to white men: if a half-caste resulted its lighter colour was attributed to the supposition that the mother had eaten the white man's flour!

In one of Firth's books on the Tikopia,[17] we find that woman is regarded simply as a repository, providing a suitable haven for the semen of the man to develop: the woman is thought to contribute nothing genetic to her children. Firth quotes one Pa Fenuatara—

> The semen is there only in the man, and when he and the woman copulate the member of the man ejaculates ... into the belly of the woman. But the semen of the woman, no! It is there in him alone. The semen of the man is there in the belly of the man, hence it is called "the house of the child in the man," that is the semen. And the house of the child in the woman is the womb.

Some primitive people believe that the egg (or the sperm) is already in the shape of a tiny person, humunculus, which then grows appropriately in the womb. The Arapesh, studied by Margaret Mead, believe that the child in the womb has a will of its own, choosing for itself the moment of birth. Once the child is born the recovery of the mother can be aided in various ways: amongst the Marquesans by an immediate bout of sexual intercourse in a nearby stream.

In *The Sexual Life of Savages* Malinowski describes the complex but utterly confused doctrines held by the Trobrianders about human physiology. It is seen that the organs of sex serve for excretion and for pleasure (in fact, as even a good few moderns do not realize, the female urethra is distinct from the genital tract). The urinary processes are not associated with the kidneys, and it is thought that water that is drunk becomes discoloured in the stomach by contact with excrement. For in this view it is in the stomach that food begins to be changed into excrement.

The eyes are regarded as the seat of desire and lust (*magila kayta*, literally "desire of copulation"). The eyes are the basis of sexual passion, and it is from the eyes that desire is carried to the brain, and thence to all parts of the body until it concentrates in the kidneys. From the kidneys, ducts (*wotuna*) lead to the male organ, and this is the tip or point (*matala*, literally "eye") of the whole system. The

olfactory sense can sometimes replace the eyes as the cause
of lust: "when a woman discards her grass petticoat in the
dark, desire may be aroused." The male and female sexual
secretions are thought to be generated in the kidneys and
have no purpose other than to lubricate the membrane and
increase pleasure.

Nothing is thought to be produced in the testes, and
questions as to whether the male fluid (*momona*) has its
source there are answered with an emphatic negative. After
all, they argue, women have no testes and yet they produce
momona. The testes are thought to be purely ornamental,
and exist to "make the penis look proper" (*bwoyna*).

The Tikopia believed that women have two wombs. If a
boy-child is growing it occupies the womb on the right, if a
girl the one on the left. When the man ejaculates, the semen
drifts into the woman's belly and thence to legs, arms, head
and body. It is thought that semen is the product of coconut cream and other fatty liquids, and is proportionate in
each person to the quantity of these substances consumed.
The buttocks are thought to be the main reservoir of
semen. As with the Trobrianders, the testicles are assigned
no functional role. Firth quotes Pa Tekaumata—

> When a man eats coconut, and eats pudding, the oil
> passes down, goes then to stay in the buttocks of the man.
> So when he sleeps with his wife, and they copulate, the
> semen descends to go into the vulva of the woman. So it is
> with the oil of birds, and the oil of fat fish, and creamy
> food. Hard food alone, when it is eaten, it has no semen.
> If he ejaculates little semen, then eats coconut, then a man
> has a great amount of semen. The semen is there in the
> buttocks. Testicles are things simply there; but a woman
> grasps the penis, that is the male organ.

The theory regarding the generation of semen involves the
choice of food. The husband is obliged to respect the totem
of his wife, and during the early years of marriage he refrains
from eating birds or fishes which are taboo to her, since they
would come to form part of his semen, and in coitus would

enter her body and bring all manner of disaster. When the man's body is weakened by age, or if copulation ceases for any other reason, then he may eat the tabooed foods once again.

Strange beliefs lead to painful rituals. Old men, for example, are circumcized for a second time in the assumption that this ritual will enable them to regain their lost potency. In some tribes circumcision has involved a deliberate incision into the penis itself, and penile flesh, as well as prepuce, may be removed.

Among the Manus husbands are not allowed to fondle their wives' breasts, a privilege that is enjoyed by the woman's cross-cousin only. Similarly in Polynesia men are expected not to caress a woman's breasts, but to concentrate on scratching their lover's face! Among the Trobrianders, albinos are considered unfit for sexual intercourse and offenders of this code have been executed. Where albino women are found to be pregnant it is sometimes assumed that an evil spirit must have done the deed. In many primitive societies taboos have existed against the remarriage of widows, on the grounds that they carry death with them. And any mention of sex, in the brother-sister relationship among the Manus, is sternly forbidden. Thus, in Mead,[14] "A father may tell his daughter that her grass skirt is awry, but her brother may not. . . ."

CHAPTER THREE

SUPERSTITION IN EARLY CIVILIZATION

In all societies superstition impinges on man's cosmogony and is intimately connected with his religious belief. Necessarily man's view of nature is also deeply influenced by his superstitious imaginings, as is his concept of himself and, for our purposes, his attitude to sex. According to Confucius, the male and female forces or principles, termed *Yang* and *Yin*, existed in a primeval chaos. Gradually the two principles separated, one going to form the heaven, the other descending to form the earth. The state of Nature was formed from the union of heaven and earth, or male and female, creating all the animals and plants and other objects of the world. It was thought that every creature owed its character to the precise proportion in which *Yang* and *Yin* were blended (M'Clatchey has stated that *Yang* is the *membrum virile* and *Yin* is the *pudendum muliebre*).

An important point of this doctrine was that *everything*, animate or not, was thought to owe its existence to the union of the male and female elements, with the male (heavenly) element the superior and the female (earthly) element the inferior participant. In due course *Yang* and *Yin* were spiritualized and sacrifices were made to them in early China as fertility deities.

In common with other ancient civilizations China had a number of phallic deities.[1] Shang-te was all-powerful and, like the tribal god of the Hebrews, seems to have been a pillar god. The spirit of thunder, Lui-Shin was another phallic god and was the equivalent to Vishnu of the Hindus, Jupiter of the Greeks, and Osiris of the Egyptians. One

of the principal nature-goddesses was Shing-moo, the holy
mother or "mother of perfect intelligence," the counterpart
of the Egyptian Isis, the Hindu Ganga, and the Greek
Demeter. The first Christian missionaries in China were
startled to find that the image of this goddess resembled
ones of the Virgin Mary and that Shingo-moo had conceived
and given birth to a saviour son while yet a virgin!

The most celebrated of all goddesses in ancient China is
Kwai-Yin, still worshipped today in the Shinto and Buddhist
faiths. According to Reed she was originally bisexual and
had a multiplicity of arms, possibly as many as a thousand.
She is the wife or consort of Shang-te, under whose guardian-
ship she occupies a throne made of the sacred Lotus. The
god and goddess are rapt in their contemplation of the
creative work of nature, symbolized in the womb of the
goddess herself, the "golden vial" replete with wondrous
treasures. Sometimes Kwai-Yin is represented as yielding a
mass of babies that seem to be growing out of her fingers and
toes and all other parts of her body; in another representation
the goddess has no less than seven heads.

In ancient Japan the same preoccupation with the reproductive principle in nature is easily discernable. In the
majority of cases the gods and goddesses were concerned
with generation, as their names show: Taka-mi-Musubi (the
high august producer), Kami-musuri (the divine producer),
Izanagi (the male who invites), and Izanami (the female
who invites). The Kunado deity, represented by a phallus,
was thought to be an antidote to all that was evil, and the
monkey-god Saruta ("whom the shameless goddess Uzume
approached in an indecent manner") had a clearly phallic
character.

The phallic deities, the *Sahe No Kami* of Shintoism and
Buddhism, were worshipped everywhere and phallic replicas
were found in city streets, in the woods and among the
mountains. Ancient Shintoism worshipped the "supreme
function" and fatherhood was everywhere recognized as the
highest mission of the gods. The phallus itself came to be
deified under the name of Konsei Myojin and associated with

all the religious paraphernalia of temples, images, and replicas of various sorts.

Temple prostitutes were common in ancient Japan, as elsewhere. Kaempfer has described a religious order of beautiful young girls called *Bikuni* or nuns, who occupied special establishments equivalent, in all but sexual philosophy, to the nunneries of Europe. The *Bikuni* were sacred harlots and it was considered a great privilege to become a member of the order, the girls being selected for their beauty and amorous capabilities from all social classes. The sacred character of such prostitution has been well established, though some early writers disliked such customs. In the *Histories* of Herodotus we find a description of the Babylonian requirement that women offer themselves once in their lives in the temple of Aphrodite. The women would journey to the temple and wait for a passing man to choose them: once a woman had been offered "sacred money" in the temple she was obliged to have sexual relations with the man in question. Herodotus, finding this religious custom "wholly shameful," observed that "tall, handsome women soon manage to get home again, but the ugly ones stay a long time before they can fulfil the condition which the law demands, some of them, indeed, as much as three or four years."

According to one authority, Dr Genchi Kato, the first reference to phallicism in ancient Japanese literature appears in the *Kogoshui* (AD 807), wherein it is stated that in a moment of anger Mitoshi-no-Kami, the god of rice, sent a plague of locusts to destroy the rice crop, and "the people offered a phallic emblem to the god as a means of appeasing him." Since that time it has been customary to offer each spring to Mitoshi a phallic effigy consisting of a carved wooden figure with a huge phallus, the aim being to ensure a plentiful rice crop in the following autumn. Everywhere the "Heavenly Root," i.e. the phallus, was worshipped at appropriate shrines. Erect objects of wood and stone, even where not obviously representations of the human penis, were "sun-stones" intended to symbolize the union of the sun and the phallus.

Shinto temples were the scenes of sexual orgies fulfilling various religious functions, similar to the Bacchanalia of ancient Rome. The phallicism in these temples is examined in two sacred books of Japan, the Kojiki and the Nihongi, which according to Scott have never been translated into English "because of their obscene nature." In 1882 C. Dresser wrote of musicians at a Shinto festival "making rude music with gongs and fifes," and of a masked actor "whose gestures would not be tolerated in England." The actor, appearing alternately as male and female, carried an "unmistakably phallic" staff. In 1911 Munro noted courtesan processions with the phallus "being then very conspicuous." Hirschfeld, writing in 1935,[2] stated that among people who still pray to phallic deities are women who are sterile or suffer from abdominal diseases, prostitutes, impotent men, brothel owners, and unhappy lovers.

In India the phallus, or Lingam, has been extensively worshipped and a wide range of phallic deities were created. The five-faced god, Punchanunu, actually Siva, was worshipped in the form of a stone placed under a tree. Morang Bura, a god of the Santals, was represented by a huge upright stone to which sacrifices were made: in tradition this deity was responsible for the formation of the earth and the creation of the first pair of human beings.

The recognition of the female principle (*Sakti*) in creation led to every Hindu deity being given a consort or wife. *Sakti* is personified by the worshippers of Siva, the generating deity responsible for the production of human beings and animals, plants and inanimate objects, in Parvati, Durga Kali or Uma. The female consort of Brahma was Sarasvati, while the consort of Vishnu was Siri. *Sakti* was also personified in the goddess Cunti!

Some Hindu sects came to worship the male element as having sole responsibility for the creation of life, whilst other groups attributed exclusive power to the female component. In the Sacred Books it is recorded that a quarrel between Mahadeva and Parvati was responsible for the division of the people into these types of worshippers. The "divine pair" had a dispute about the relative importance of the two sexes in generating animate beings, and each resolved to create a new race of people. The race produced by Mahadeva became known as the Lingajas ("their intellects were dull, their bodies feeble, their limbs distorted, and their complexions of different hues"). By contrast the Yonijas, created by Parvati, adored the female power only (they "were all well shaped, with sweet aspects and fine complexions"). The two races came into conflict and the Lingajas were defeated in battle: Parvati interposed to prevent Mahadeva destroying the Yonijas "with the fire of his eyes."

In accordance with this legend two sects of worshippers were represented in ancient India—the Lingayats, worshipping the Lingam as the sole symbol of generation; and the Yonijas, worshipping the female power whose symbol is the Yoni. The Lingayats (also called Lingawauts, Saivas and Jangams) wore a phallic emblem on some part of their dress or body. The emblem, made of gold, silver, copper or beryl, was in many cases identical with the *fascinum* of the ancient Romans and the *jettatura* of modern Italy. The Vaishnavas and Saktas (followers of Vishnu) carried similar emblems. By contrast the Yonijas used an emblem in the shape of a naked girl or of the Yoni (*pudendum muliebre*) itself.

In addition to these two central sects a large number of subsidiary groups also flourished in ancient India and were detectable in modern times. One sect, called the Jougies, was described in the eighteenth century by Hamilton.[3] He records the sect's condemnation of clothes and worldly riches ("some deny themselves" even "a bit of cloth about their loins" and delight "in nastiness and a holy obscenity, with a great show of sanctity"), and describes one "sanctified rascal"—

seven foot high, and his limbs well proportioned, with a large turban of his own hair wreathed about his head, and his body bedawbed with ashes and water, sitting quite naked under the shade of a tree, with a *pudenda* like an ass, and a hole bored through his prepuce, with a large gold ring fixed in the hole.

E

Large numbers of young married women revered the chap
and took him devoutly in their hands to kiss him, in particular
his phallus, whilst its "bawdy owner stroked their silky heads
muttering some filthy prayers for their prolification." A
majority of Hindu phallic worshippers believed in the joint
responsibility of the male and female elements in the creation of life, and Lingam and Yoni were applauded in such
sects with equal devotion. A sect of Brahmans, the Seyvias,
worshipped the phallic deity Eswara, who was represented
in his temples, according to one observer, "under a very
immodest shape, expressing commerce of the sexes." According to tradition, a Moniswara, visiting the temple of Eswara
at a time when the god was engaged in sexual intercourse
with Parvati, was refused entry, and broke out into an impre-
cation that whoever should worship Eswara under the above
mentioned shape might receive greater advantage than if he
worshipped the god under his proper image. Hence the
"scandalous and indecent images" under which Eswara came
to be worshipped.

Sometimes an erect phallus in stone was set upon a
pedestal as a centrepiece in appropriate ritual. In the Great
Pagoda of Madura the deity is represented as a block of
black granite, four feet in height, and conical in shape, with
a human face at the top with a golden arch over it. Such
Lingams were constructed in durable materials so that they
would be permanent: in the holy *Shastras* it is stated that
once a Lingam has been fixed to the ground it should remain
there forever to preserve the sanctity of the symbol. Even to
move the object from one place to another would be
regarded as an act of desecration.

Because Mount Kailasa in the Tibetan Himalayas is
thought to resemble a Lingam in shape, both the god Siva
and his consort Parvati are thought to reside there; and
devotees of these divine beings make pilgrimages to the
sacred mountain. Similarly a ring, a circle, a cleft, etc, came
to represent the feminine element, and each was termed a
Yoni. In Moor's *Hindu Pantheon* a cleft rock is described,
situated at the extremity of a promontory called Malabar
Point to which worshippers journeyed "for the purpose of

regeneration by the efficacy of a passage through this sacred type." In the same work we are told that Ragonaut Rao frequently passed his body through the cleft on Malabar Hill and benefited greatly by such regeneration. Similarly, it is stated, Sivaji, the founder of the Mahrata state, ventured secretly upon the island of Bombay, at a time when discovery would have meant his ruin, to avail himself of the effects of the regenerative transit.

One idea, it appears, was to construct of pure gold a life-size statue of the female principle, either in the shape of a woman or a cow. The person wanting regeneration was enclosed in the statue and then dragged out through the genital tract. Practical difficulties in carrying out this procedure induced the priests to decree that it was sufficient to make an image of the sacred Yoni, through which the individual could pass: hence rings, clefts, triangles, circles, etc. Stones with circular holes in them, like the "holed stones" of Ireland and Cornwall, were employed for this purpose.

Where Lingam and Yoni were worshipped in union it was generally thought necessary to have some durable image or representation. Thus an upright emblem of the phallus was sometimes set upon an *argha* or shell-shaped Yoni, a double symbol sometimes termed the *Pulleiar*. In Seely's *The Wonders of Alora* (1824) there is a description of joint worship of Lingam and Yoni: the base of the stone Lingam is inserted in the Yoni. Seely, though capable of describing such things in detail observed that "this symbol is grossly indecent, and abhorrent to every moral feeling. . . ."

The open eroticism in much of Hindu religion has brought condemnation from many observers of nervous disposition. Seely notes roundly that "there is nothing too depraved or lascivious for the Hindu mind to contemplate and describe." In similar vein, Signor Pietro della Valle, a seventeenth-century traveller, visited a temple dedicated to the idol Virena Deuru: many of the figures depicted in the building represented "dishonest actions." He observes:

One was of a woman, lifting up her clothes before, and

showing that which modesty obliged her to cover. Another was of a man and woman kissing, the man holding his hand on the woman's breasts: another had a man and a woman naked, with their hands on one another's shameful parts, those of the man being of excessive greatness, and sundry such representations fit indeed for such a temple.

According to another observer, a certain Captain Hamilton, the temples of the phallic god Gopalsami were decorated with obscene effigies of men and women in "indescribably indecent" postures and of demons with immense genital organs. Rajendralala Mitra recorded that in the temples of Orissa were depictions of "human couples in the most disgustingly obscene positions," and at the Great Temple of Puri "a few of the human figures are disgustingly obscene." John Fryer, writing in 1698, describes pagodas in Madras devoted to phallic worship: on the walls of the temples were "obscene images, where Aretino might have furnished his fancy for his bawdy postures."

What Scott considered one of the most "extraordinary and repulsive" of the fertility rites was connected with the sacrifice of a horse to the deity. An animal selected for the purpose was allowed to roam at large for a year before being offered in sacrifice by being secured to a post and then smothered. A woman was then compelled to lie down next to the corpse of the animal, and both woman and animal were covered with a large opaque sheet. In the words of Tawney (1924): "In that position she performed a very obscene act with the horse symbolizing the transmission to her of its great powers of fertility." This sort of activity, and all manner of open eroticism were put down by the British Raj but there can be no doubt that much secret sex worship continued under British rule of India. Towards the end of the nineteenth century, for example, thousands of pilgrims assembled for the annual Mela at the temple of Vaidyanath in Bengal. And in a number of notorious nineteenth century court cases (e.g. the Maharaj libel case in

1862) many instances of phallic worship were divulged by witnesses.

Plutarch records that the statue of Osiris in ancient Egypt had the phallus to signify his procreative and prolific power: Isis, his wife, symbolized the female principle, and both gods were phallic in character. One writer noted that the Egyptians worshipped "things as gods that they might well have blushed to name." According to legend, Osiris was killed by his brother Typhon who then dismembered the corpse and distributed the pieces in various places. Isis set herself the task of recovering the portions of her mutilated husband's body. With the exception of the genitals, which had been thrown into the Nile, she succeeded in her task and for every section of the body recovered Isis caused a statue to be built and worshipped. Because the genitals had never been regained Isis insisted that the statues of these organs should receive particular adulation. On account of its virility and productiveness the ox came to be the representative of Osiris and as such was duly worshipped. (It is interesting that many other gods in ancient legend, e.g. the Phoenician god Camillus, were killed and castrated, their genitals being carried away.)

In addition to being a sun-god, Osiris came to symbolize the river Nile. Associated with virility he was invariably depicted, in statutary or otherwise, with the phallus fully exposed and erect. Egyptian women carried images of Osiris about with them, and at religious festivals they carried in triumphal procession larger images with movable phalli of abnormal size and proportions. In some instances a man was substituted for the image and was expected to be naked and lascivious. Such men were highly honoured by the people. Of such men De Thevenot wrote in 1687:

It is no fiction that many women, who cannot be got with child, kiss their Priapus with great veneration, nay sometimes they procure a Great-belly by them. There was one of these blades heretofore carried a great stone hanging at his *glans*, and the women heartily kissed it for a Big Belly.

On the death of Isis she too was deified and came to be worshipped in the shape of a cow. The cow image was later transferred to that of a woman, who became the representative of the goddess. The image had immense genitals and bore on her head the horns of a cow. In some instances Isis has been depicted holding in her hand a representation of the female womb. Sometimes the representation took the form of a sistrum, the Egyptian symbol of virginity or immaculateness, Isis clearly being the forerunner of the Virgin Mary of Christianity. The sistrum was carried in phallic processions to the gay accompaniment of phallic songs.

Osiris and Isis were not the only phallic deities of ancient Egypt. In addition there was Khem, god of generation and bearing consequent responsibility for the perpetuation of the race. His consort, the goddess Maut, was termed simply "the Mother." Another phallic deity was Min, whose image was found in all parts of ancient Egypt. The Egyptian god, Ammon, was the husband of his mother, and boasted of the fact (Odin, the Norse god, has been referred to as the husband of one of his own daughters). The Egyptian dynastic rulers often incurred incestuous relations, so it is likely that the characters of the gods were fashioned on the basis of operating social conventions. It has often been pointed out that any society that traces its origins back to an original pair (Isis and Osiris in Egyptian legend, Adam and Eve in Judeo-Christian legend) must assume incest between parents and children or between brothers and sisters. Cain and Abel presumably had no other way of reproducing their kind. In Egypt the various incestuous practices eventually died out, with periodic revivals, the last of which was under the Ptolemies who are said to have practised marriage between brother and sister for three hundred years "without noticeably bad physical effects."[4]

As well as the all-pervasive influence of Osiris and Isis in Egypt a number of lesser deities, of lower status to Khem and Maut, were assigned particular roles in the sexual and reproductive realm.[5] Thus some goddesses were particularly concerned with obstetrics and gynaecology. One deity was a general obstetrician, and one had special charge of the birth house where a woman could go at the onset of labour. A third deity was supposed to take charge of the hot stones over which a woman would crouch during labour. And yet another was primarily interested in the feeding of infants. One deity was assigned the task of ensuring the proper developement of the foetus, and ancient paintings show that the body and personality were prepared by different gods before being combined and given life. Inevitably, Egyptian doctors were priests also.

Many paintings and papyri from ancient Egypt are still in existence and throw light on medical practices and beliefs of the time. Often women doctors are shown conducting operations and midwives are seen with their patients: the physical body is shown and also what is imagined to be the soul. The Egyptians, in common with members of many Eastern religions and some of the early Christian fathers, believed that the soul arrived late in pregnancy and that the foetus became truly alive only when it started to move in the womb.

In the Syrian temple of Hierapolis, for instance, two enormous phalli stood on either side of the door and were regarded as representing the generative organs of the deity or creator with which he impregnated the heavens, the earth and the waters. And in the Middle East and elsewhere phallic worship often involved prolonged orgies (in Scott's words) "of the most decadent nature." In the rites of Pelarga a young woman was impregnated as an offering to the goddess, and in Old Russia, at the meetings between the Skoptzis and the Christs, the Holy Virgin was often represented by a young woman involved in licentious ritual. In a number of ancient societies women were induced to pray at the feet of a bull-image for fertility and other blessings. Bull worship existed in Greece, Rome, Egypt, Assyria and many other places. Fertility rites celebrated at Bury St Edmunds in the late eighteenth century involved leading a white bull in procession through the main streets of the town, attended by monks and a crowd of townspeople. A woman walked at the side of the bull, stroking him until the procession reached the church door, whereupon the woman entered the church, paid her vows at the altar of St Edmund, kissed the stone, and entreated the blessing of a child.

Another area of sexual superstition in early civilization concerns love potions or aphrodisiacs.[6] In savage societies various devices were employed to stimulate sexual appetite or procure the attentions of a loved one. The use of a placenta, for example, was commonplace in ancient communities and persisted through various societies up to modern times: if a girl could contrive to induce her lover to unwittingly consume part of a placenta, preferably the girl's own, preserved by her diligent mother, then his undying adoration could be assured. Herbs were also a ready standby in the absence of a suitable afterbirth. The Roman poet Ovid was well aware of the use of aphrodisiacs but seemed to consider their use somewhat unfair ("Love is wrongfully acquired by herbs, which should be won by merit and beauty"). Pliny the Elder treated love potions with contempt, and dismissed a Thessalian plant from his encyclopedia for the Romans because "it would be a mere loss of time to describe, seeing that it is only used as an ingredient of philters."

A Sumerian, living in southern Mesopotamia four thousand years ago, employed a priest to recover his lost love, and the incantation used for the purpose was transmitted to the Babylonians and Assyrians on a clay tablet now in the University of Pennsylvania Museum. Magicians in ancient India offered enchantments for every amorous occasion, and the sacred Vedas contain many examples of love magic. Sometimes the spells were multi-purpose: for a woman whose husband was growing indifferent it would clearly be advisable to use spells capable of stimulating a man's love, of increasing a woman's beauty, and of destroying a possible rival. The *Kama-Sutra* of Vatsyayana recommended the use of love magic for making human love sublime; the *Ananga-Ranga* of Kalyanamalla, dated to the fifteenth century, offered to teach all the magic that is needed to win, hold, and enjoy the opposite sex; and in a rather different spirit, in the Sanskrit epic the *Mahabharata*, composed two thousand years ago, a certain woman named Draupadi, able to keep five husbands happy at the same time, condemned the use of love charms on husbands (at the same time she did not deny the efficacy of such methods).

In ancient Greece, influenced by Asia and Egypt, there is frequent reference to love magic. Even such reflective men as Euripides and Plato mention in their writings the use of love incantations and philters. Socrates is recorded as saying jokingly "I have other mistresses who will allow me to depart from them neither by day or by night; learning from me, as they do, love charms and incantations." And witches from Thessaly and Phrygia were famous among the Greeks as dispensers of love charms; from such women, or from retired prostitutes setting up in another type of business, love charms were easy to obtain.

According to Aristotle a woman was brought before the judges because a love philter had inadvertently killed her lover. She pleaded that she had only wished to revive a dying love, and so the judges acquitted her. Sappho of Lesbos suggested that magic could overcome homosexuality.

The ancient Roman had little doubt about the efficacy of love magic. From the fifth century BC the law of the Twelve Tables prescribed death for the worker of magic spells. In 939 BC the praetor Cornelius Scipio Hispalus forced foreign magicians to leave Italy; yet in the last years of the republic miracle workers of every sort were prolific in Rome. Eventually, with the growing power of the Christian Church, magic became heresy, and an edict of Constantine invoked the death penalty for any magician who entered a private home to practise his profession.

Juvenal, a first-century satirist, reproved Roman women for dosing their husbands with love potions from Thessaly which only caused premature senility, dizziness and loss of memory. Lucretius, author of the poem *De Rerum Natura*, is said on scanty evidence to have gone mad and committed suicide because of a love potion administered to him by his wife.

Philostratus, writing in the third century, observed that

lovers are addicted above all others to magic, and that the disease from which lovers suffer renders them particularly liable to delusions. In Lucian we find a Greek courtesan named Bacchis begging a Syrian witch to help her recover an unfaithful lover. The witch demanded salt, sulphur, a torch, seven coins, a bowl of wine, and something associated with the lover such as an item of clothing or a lock of hair. Then the witch drank the wine, pocketed the coins, and threw salt and sulphur on the burning torch. Then spinning a magic wheel she gave an incantation that Bacchis thought outlandish. Greek men would take a bit of clothing or a trinket belonging to a girl, pay a witch to say spells over it, and bury the enchanted object in the earth beneath the threshold of the girl's door, where she must pass over it and be moved to love.

Similarly magical techniques were employed by the young pages and squires of medieval Europe, as recorded by the French historian Jules Michelet. If one fancied a girl it was necessary to collect her nail parings, hairs from her comb, and threads and scraps torn from her garments. These scraps were more susceptible to enchantment if unwashed and soiled with traces of sweat.

A famous aphrodisiac described by Pliny is a plant called *thelygonon* whose seeds were said to resemble testicles. Theophrastus declared that there was a plant which, held in the hand, had enabled a man to achieve sexual relations seventy times in one night, but forgot to name the plant! The Chinese valued the aromatic root of ginseng (*panax schinseng*) as an aphrodisiac. Ancient Hebrews appear to have used caper berries (*capparis spinosa*) for sexual stimulation: when the preacher of Ecclesiastes (12:5) describes the symptom of old age he speaks in the King James translation of the time "when ... desire shall fail," a passage which, in the original Hebrew, reads "when ... the caper berry shall fail."

The two aphrodisiacs most valued in antiquity, mandragora and cantharides, acted as drugs, if not as love potions: the first is a dangerous soporific, the second a violent irritant to skin and mucus membranes. Mandragora, or mandrake, is a member of the potato family and contains the alkaloids

atropine and scopolmine, and in large doses can cause
mental confusion and death. Theophrastus, in the fourth
century BC, recommended mandragora root, scraped and
soaked in vinegar, as an aphrodisiac and a cure for sleep-
lessness. According to this authority the plant must be
gathered only after drawing three circles about it with a
sword and facing towards the west while an assistant
dances in a circle reciting magic formulas. Pliny, noting that
the roots of the mandragora might have the form of either
male or female genitalia, repeated the instructions of
Theophrastus for uprooting the plant, and advised against
digging with the wind blowing directly into the face. Dio-
scorides, in the first century AD, included mandragora
among aphrodisiacs and urged the use of mandragora wine
as a surgical anaesthetic: the wine was sometimes given to
those about to be crucified or hung. The Egyptians called
mandragora "Phallus of the Field," and Julian the Apostate
mentioned its power when praising Callixena's devotion to
her religion—"Who can prefer in a woman conjugal love to
piety, without being thought to have taken large draughts of
mandragora?" And the Arabs called mandragora roots
"Devil's Testicles." Some primitive peoples have thought that
the mandragora root came to resemble either a male or
female figure in all its details, and that the root gave a pierc-
ing human shriek when being pulled from the earth. Diggers
were advised to go forth on a Friday before sunrise after
closing the ears with cotton and sealing the cotton with
pitch or wax. The root was loosened and tied to the tail of
a dog: a piece of bread thrown to the animal made it leap
forward, whereupon the root screamed and the dog was
expected to die instantly.

Cantharides is mentioned as an aphrodisiac by Aristotle,
who also recommended oil of peppermint for the same purpose. The active principle of cantharides, cantharidin, is contained in the dried bodies of the blister beetle, and in the
bodies of other beetles of the same family, such as the Telini
"fly" of India. Ancient doctors and priests suffocated the
beetles in the fumes of hot vinegar prior to drying and
powdering their bodies.

If cantharides is swallowed in any but the smallest doses, a destructive reaction occurs in the mucus membranes of mouth, throat, stomach, and intestines. In addition there can be damage to the kidneys, ulceration of the bladder, and erosion of the urethra. Blood may be vomited or passed out from the bowels. A state of priapism may also result, which may explain to some extent the reputation of the drug as an aphrodisiac. A too large dose can cause agonizing death in sixteen to twenty-four hours.

The dangers of cantharides have long been recognized but the substance has been widely used as an aphrodisiac from ancient times to the present day. In Greece women inserted a piece of lint treated with cantharides into the vagina both as an aphrodisiac and to procure abortion. The drug was also recommended by physicians for a variety of ailments. Pliny told the story of Cossinus, an intimate of the Emperor Nero, who was suffering from a disfiguring skin disease. A famous physician from Egypt prescribed a potion of cantharides and killed the patient.

In the Middle Ages cantharides was widely used as a love potion. A fashionable bathhouse in eighteenth century Paris specialized in perfumed pre-nuptial baths, followed by a massage of cantharides and a meal of truffles cooked in champagne. The Marquis de Sade fed bonbons containing cantharides to a group of prostitutes in a Marseilles brothel.

Drugs, which at least had some demonstrable effects, were a common form of aphrodisiac in the ancient world. Great claims were made for alcohol, opium, hashish and all the rest, and though the claims were certainly exaggerated some efficacy, if only in lowering inhibitions, was achieved.

One technique of attracting a man employed a magic wheel having four spokes to which a bird was tied. Then the wheel was spun quickly with a cord or whip, an activity that was supposed to make a man in question feel love pangs for the hapless girl who had instigated the event. Some spells made use of the bones of the dead and it became necessary to visit tombs in the dead of night to gather together the appropriate equipment. Horace[7] describes the scene of a spell on the Esquiline. Two old women, Canidia and Sagana, chant their spells with mournful howlings. The shades of the dead are invoked and a trench is furrowed in the earth into which is poured the blood of a black lamb. Dogs and serpents from the underworld gather round the unholy pair to witness the final stage of the spell: the melting of a wax doll, representing the beloved, in the fire. Alas things go wrong and in their flight Sagana loses her wig and Canidia her false teeth.

A preoccupation in many Greek and Roman writers was the control of conception. In the first century AD, Pliny the Elder suggested that if one took two small worms out of the body of a certain spider and attached them in a piece of deer-skin to a woman's body before sunrise, then she would not conceive. Some ancient writers have declared that if a woman spat three times into a frog's mouth she would not conceive for a year, and that a jasper pebble clasped in the hand during coitus would prevent conception.[8] St Albert the Great (c. 1225–74) is said to have advised eating bees for the same purpose. Soranos of Ephesus, described by Professor Himes as the most brilliant gynaecologist of antiquity, discouraged the use of magic potions and amulets to prevent pregnancy and urged instead pessaries impregnated with honey. Aetios of Amida suggested, perhaps less rationally, that a man should wash his penis in vinegar or brine and that a woman should wear a cat's testicle in a tube across her navel.

Similar oddities can be found in many other ancient writings. In old Sanskrit sources recommendations include rubbing the navel or the soles of the feet with salves made of certain plants. There is also mention of vaginal medication with rocksalt dipped in oil (Fryer notes that an 8·5 per cent solution of table salt is a very effective spermicide, but that rock salt used permanently as a pessary has been found to cause dyspareunia—pain during sexual intercourse—and sterility). Sanskrit writers knew about the more rational technique of *coitus obstructus* in which the thumb and forefinger of either partner are pressed against the base of the penis as ejaculation begins, causing the semen to be sent into the bladder, from which it is later expelled during urination. The Talmud, the ancient body of Hebrew law, also has a word or two about contraception. In addition to the drinking of potions to prevent conception, women are urged to twist their bodes violently after copulation, an activity that may well be puzzling to an uninitiated partner.

Islamic physicians suggested, as tampons, pomegranate pulp with alum, rock salt, and cabbage leaves with tar. In *The Perfumed Garden* techniques to be used by the man include rubbing the penis with rock salt, tar, onion juice, and oil of balsam. Less plausible methods of avoiding conception including sneezing after coitus, raising the thigh, and avoiding simultaneous orgasms. One Islamic authority suggested that a woman should exhale sharply at the moment of the man's ejaculation, on the principle that the increased intra-abdominal pressure would push out the cervical mucus along with the semen. The ancient Chinese appear to have relied on a mixture of magic potions, and abortion when the magic failed.

In some early European communities women would sit on a number of fingers according to the number of years they wished to remain childless. For the same purpose seeds and leaves of fruitless trees, notably the willow, would be infused and drunk as tea. Even in modern times German women believed that willow tea would make them sterile. Another old European superstition is that coitus without passion does not lead to conception. In ancient Greece and Rome a whole range of gods and goddesses could be appealed to to prevent conception, to cause it (i.e. to alleviate sterility), and to banish a whole host of sexual problems.

In Greece, Hermes was a name given both to the penis and to Mercury, the phallic god. The deity Priapus, presiding over all matters of fertility, was generally shown with an enormous phallus, and in his temples all manner of sexual activity took place. In one story the Greek men of Lampsacus, jealous of the sexual capacity of Priapus, expelled him from the island: the women, distressed by this unfortunate turn of events, prayed incessantly to the gods, with the result that a loathsome disease visited all the male members of the community. The oracle of Dodona declared that the disease could not be banished until the god Priapus be recalled and given suitable reverence.

The images used in the worship of Priapus took on a number of shapes. In some cases the figure was simply a human head attached to an enormous phallus: in other instances the head surmounted a pedestal from which the gigantic erect organ protruded.

These priapi, as the models were termed, could be found everywhere. They were often used as signposts or for marking boundaries. They were to be seen in the gardens of Rome and were thought to have a beneficent influence upon the fertility of the soil. Sometimes the image of the god was hewn out of a living tree. Smaller priapi were carried about by worshippers and worn on their bodies. The sculpture of ancient Greece and the medals and coins then in use testify well to the persistent interest in phallicism at that time. Often coitus was depicted, and since the medals and coins were issued by the state authority they give a clear indication of existing culture.

Zeus himself, supreme in the Greek pantheon, was portrayed as the suitor and benefactor of a vast number of mortal and immortal women and girls, a circumstance leading to inevitable jealousy of his wife and sister, Hera. On one occasion Zeus carried off the beautiful Trojan boy, Ganymede, and thus sanctioned the love of boys on the heights of Olympus.

In memory of the sacred marriage of Zeus and Hera, glorified in poetry, spring-time festivals were celebrated with flowers and garlands: the image of Hera dressed in bridal attire was carried round and a bridal bed woven with flowers was prepared for her.

Greek mythology is full of the amorous adventures of gods and goddesses: Apollo loved Avadne and many others; Actaeon, the hunter, spied upon Artemis while she was bathing, and was afterwards turned into a stag by the enraged goddess and torn to pieces by his own dogs; Aphrodite became the goddess that grants and asks for love; and with all these and numerous other deities were associated regular festivals of licentious abandon. Love-feasts dedicated to Aphrodite took place on the island of Cyprus and else-where. The image of the goddess was bathed by women and girls in the holy sea, after which they themselves bathed in the river under myrtle bushes in preparation for the coming orgies.

In Aphrodite were combined all the amorous qualities. She was often depicted wearing a seductive girdle which Homer thought could even infatuate the mind of the wise. Poets and sculptors glorified her attributes—eyes and neck, breasts and limbs, and even what Hans Licht feels obliged to denote "that portion of the human back which, in present-day good society, is unnamable."[9] Thus Greeks worshipped their Aphrodite Kallipygos, the goddess "with beautiful buttocks." In the Museo Nazionale in Naples, in a little room named Veneri, visitors can see a bare statue of Aphrodite: she is lifting her dress and glancing over her shoulder at her charms.

Another amorous goddess was Eos (Aurora), the goddess of dawn, whom Homer calls rosy-fingered. Eos loves every-thing that is beautiful, especially young men, and she forc-ibly seizes anyone who arouses her passion. Thus she carried off Cleitus, Cephalus, Orion, and Tithonus. Selene, the moon-goddess, also had amorous inclinations and had once slept with Zeus, to whom she bore the beautiful Pandia. Best known of all is her love for Endymion whom she surprised while he slept in the wooded hills of Latmos, and after that blessed him every night with her love.

The giant Orion had a more violent disposition: in a fit of drunkenness he violated the daughter (or wife) of his guest and friend, Oenopion, king of Chios. For this he is blinded by his father but gropes his way towards the beams of the sun which eventually restore his sight. On another occasion he lusted after Artemis whereupon the goddess sent a scor-pion to kill the giant.

Inevitably the gods and goddesses were involved in human ritual and festival. In Greece weddings usually took place in winter, preferably on the first day of January, the day of one of the festivals of Gamelia, a surname of Juno. On the morn-ing of the wedding day animal sacrifices were made to Zeus and Hera and libations of wine poured. In the afternoon both bride and bridegroom were separately given ceremonial baths in the holy water of some sacred fountain. With the rising of Hesperus, the evening star, the bridegroom would drive his bride home in a mule-cart. In Sparta a girl's hair was cut short on her wedding day and she was dressed like a man. She was then taken into an unlit room and made to lie on a hard straw-mattress. No marriage feast was provided. The husband, who had dined at his Messing Club, arrived later, groped his way in, and returned to barracks an hour or two afterwards. Plutarch records that the young husband "did the same thing again and again; he spent the day with his comrades, slept with them at night, and visited his bride only secretly and with circumspection, feeling ashamed and being afraid that someone in her house might see him."

Elsewhere in ancient Greece the wedding-banquet was customary, and was generally given in the house of the bride's father. Sesame cakes, to which (according to Menander) a fructifying influence was ascribed, were a common delicacy. Sometimes a beautiful naked boy, adorned with thorns and oak-leaves, would carry round a plate with pastry for the guests, at the same time crying out "I have avoided the bad and found what is better."

After the couple had arrived at their home in the ox-cart the axle was sometimes burnt to ensure that the young wife might never wish to leave her husband's house. If a widower married again he himself took no part in the marriage procession, but waited at home for his bride who was brought to him by a friend.

Wedding ceremonies were paralleled in ancient Greece by rituals of a more bizarre kind. Temple orgies were commonplace. In various parts of the ancient world it is highly likely that necrophiliac rites were conducted, a probability that may be deduced from the Greek myth where Achilles chose to have sexual intercourse with the corpse of the Amazon queen Penthesilia after he had slain her.

As in more primitive societies, superstition in Greece can be found not only in attitudes to major and minor deities

F

and in beliefs about the efficacy of ceremonial performance, but also in erroneous ideas as to matters of fact. The school of Hippocrates thought that the womb had two chambers, males being conceived on the right side and females on the left. And the uterus was even regarded by the Greeks as a separate animal. Thus Plato states in the *Timaeus:*

> That part of the woman which is called the womb, being an animal desirous of generation, if it become unfruitful for a long time turns indignant, and wandering all over the body stops the passages of the spirits and the respiration, and occasions the most extreme anxiety and all sorts of diseases.

It was thought that when the womb travelled upwards it would approach the heart, liver and stomach causing any number of diseases. The anxiety sometimes resulting from the travels of the womb was given the special name of "suffocation of the womb" or hysteria. The condition was thought to be most common in virgins, since their wombs were thought to be lighter than those of childbearing women, and the lightness enabled the organ to wander more freely. In a hysterical fit the womb was thought to have been drawn up near the liver by some mysterious attraction. There it would remain until it pumped itself full of blood and descended again. To draw the womb back more quickly the woman should be given vile things to sniff at the same time her vagina was fumigated with sweet and pleasant smelling substances. In such a fashion should the wandering womb be attracted to its proper location. The idea that the womb moved about in this way was accepted for many centuries. In the event of a prolapse, the only way in which the womb could actually shift its position, the smelling technique was employed in reverse, i.e. the vagina was subjected to evil-smelling substances to drive the womb away.

Superstition about aphrodisiacs was widespread. According to Pliny the sap of the flea-wort was effective in securing the birth of boys: all the parents had to do was to drink the sap three times while fasting for forty days! Glaucias ascribes the same effect to the thistle. Agnus was thought to cause weakness in the sexual impulse, and thus was strewn over the beds by nervous women during the Thesmophoria. Conversely, according to Xenocrates, the sap of mallows, as well as three of its roots bound together, excited the sexual passion of women. And according to Discorides men must eat the larger root of the "boy-cabbage," if they wish to beget boys, and women the smaller, if they wanted girls. If they drank it fresh in goat's milk, the sexual desire was heightened; if they ate it dry then sexual passion would diminish. Satyrium was thought to have a stimulating effect if carried in the hand, and its root was thought to have the same effect as "boy-cabbage." If pesoluta was laid under a couple it made them impotent; whereas the root of cyclamen served as an amulet to accelerate childbirth, or it might cause an early abortion if a woman inadvertently trod on it. A twelve-day impotence resulted from drinking "sea-roses" (water-lilies), and southernwood could be used to heighten the sexual urge and to counteract charms intended to prevent conception. If asparagus root were worn as an amulet the wearer became barren.

In Pliny we find that the ashes of the plant brya mixed with the urine of an ox made one impotent; and according to magicians of the day the ashes could also be mixed with the urine of a eunuch. The plant telephilon (poppy) was used as a device in love-oracles, according to Theocritus one of its leaves was laid in the palm and struck sharply with the hand; if a loud crack resulted that was a good omen.

To protect oneself against the "evil wolf" (haemorrhage between the muscles of the buttocks), it was necessary to put absinthium (vermuth) on the posterior. And the right testicle of an ass worn in a bracelet would increase one's sexual capacities. Again in Pliny we find that a woman will bear boys if she eats the testicles, womb or rennet of a hare. Eating the foetus of a hare was said to cure barrenness for ever. The pangs of childbirth could be eased by bringing a cock to the pregnant woman or by touching her hips with the placental skin of a dog, which had not come into contact with the earth. If a woman ate a cock's testicle immediately after conception she could be sure of having a boy. To urinate where a dog had done so would make one impotent.

A superstition about the hyena was that it changed its sex every year, a notion supported by Pliny and attacked by Aristotle. And the sexual attributes of animals were also relevant to human disease: a female crab pounded in a mortar and ground with fine salt and water after the full moon could be used to cure cancerous ulcers of the womb. If a woman carried a mullus (an edible sea-fish) her menstrual blood lost its poisonous effect. It was also believed that the raven made a habit of having sexual intercourse with women with its beak: thus if one was brought into the house of a pregnant woman the result would be a difficult labour, and if a pregant woman ate a raven's egg she would miscarry through the mouth. If, alternately, she ate veal roasted with the plant aristolochia at the time of conception she would bear a boy. And Pliny also thought that cow's milk promoted conception.

If a woman exposed her genitals she could break magic spells, so an image of the vulva was often carried round by superstitious women. The exposure of the organ was thought to be particularly efficacious against hail, bad weather, and storms at sea; and the magical effect of exposure was heightened if the woman was menstruating at the time. Exposure of the female genitals at the time of menstruation was also useful in destroying vermin and in promoting agricultural growth.

The urine of a menstruating woman was also feared and held capable of counteracting magical charms. In the *Geoponica* Hierocles is said to have preferred the urine of a man to that of even menstruating woman in the case of certain horses' complaints. The slave of a friend of Porphyry understood the language of birds, until his mother urinated in his ear while he was asleep, so depriving him of the gift. Pliny suggests that the power of urine is intensified if one spits into it at the moment it is voided. A drop of urine placed on the crown of the head was thought instantly to cure the bite of the centipede; and for snake-bites one could drink one's own urine or that of a boy not yet at puberty.

Faeces were thought to be less powerful than urine, but when baked they could be used as a cure for various ailments. The excrement of a new-born child was sometimes introduced into the uterus to ensure fertility. Human milk also had healing properties, and a dog that had once tasted the milk of a woman who had recently had a son would never go mad. A person treated with a salve composed of the milk of mother and daughter enjoyed life-long immunity against affections of the eye. Many of these folk cures were in use in Europe until modern times.

Much of the superstition in ancient Greece was conveyed to Rome. The names of the gods were changed but the same focus on phallic phenomena can easily be detected. Scott describes Mutinus, a deity to all intents and purposes the same as Priapus of the Greeks (a similar Roman deity is referred to as Mutunus Tutunus by Otto Kiefer in *Sexual Life in Ancient Rome*[10]). An attempt has been made by some scholars to refer the stem of *Mutunus* to *mentula,* the male sexual organ, but the derivation is not certain. What is clear is that this deity was thought to officiate at marriages and to aid all manner of sexual disability. Lactantius wrote that "Tutinus (*sic*) also is honoured: brides seat themselves on this god's genital member in order to make the first offering of their virginity to the god." The temples dedicated to Mutunus (or Mutinus) were decorated with pictorial representations of the phallus and of men and animals engaged in coitus. Similarly, various life-sized nudes engaged in sexual intercourse were painted by the finest Roman artists upon the walls of the Imperial Banqueting Hall in the famous "Golden House" of Nero.

A whole range of Roman deities were assigned tasks of supervising man's sexual activities. Augustine wrote critically of Virginiensis, Subigus, Prema, Pertunda, Venus and Priapus. Juno was the guardian of woman's sexual functions and the deity for marriage in particular: she even has a different name for each function she is intended to supervise —thus as Iterduca she brings home the bride, as Unxia or Cinxia she superintends the anointing of the bride, as Pronuba she is the bridesmaid, and as Lucina she attends the birth of the child. The god Janus was expected to be present at sexual intercourse "in order to open the way for the conception of the seed, when the fruit of the body is conceived." Saturn was thought to protect the seed of the husband.

The cult of Venus (Aphrodite) had a number of paradoxical functions. On the one hand, for instance, this goddess was the guardian of honourable marriage; on the other, she became the goddess of *meretrices*, harlots. In some sense Venus was also regarded as the mother of the Roman nation. After his famous victory at Pharsalus, Caesar consecrated a sanctuary to Venus and gave her the permanent title of Venus Genetrix, the divine mother of the descendants of Aeneas. Caesar himself claimed descent from Venus ("The Julian clan, to which my house belongs, is sprung from Venus").

One interesting form of the worship of Venus is where she appears under the name of Verticordia. In 114 BC, three Vestal virgins were condemned to death for transgressing with Roman knights the stern law against sexual intercourse. To atone for their misdeeds a shrine was erected to Venus Verticordia in the hope that she would turn the hearts of women and girls against licentiousness and towards chastity. Hence the name *Verticordia*, meaning turner of hearts. Under this title Venus came to be worshipped especially by married women and a festival took place on the first of April. The goddess of harlots had a special day set aside on April 23, a day also used for the love festival of male prostitutes in ancient Rome.

The god Liber, originally an old Roman patron of growth and fertility, became associated with the Greek importation Dionysus. In various parts of Italy Liber was the subject of phallic cults: a large wooden phallus was carried on a cart about the fields and through the city, and was eventually crowned by a matron. Augustine describes the festival with typical Christian rancour—

That shameful part of the body was, during the festival of Liber, placed with great pomp on wagons ... a whole month was dedicated to Liber. During it, all the citizens used the most disgraceful words until the phallus had been carried across the market place and put to rest again. It was necessary that the most honourable of all matrons should publicly place a wreath on that disgraceful effigy ... the evil eye had to be repelled from the fields by compelling a married woman to do in public that which not even a harlot might do under the eyes of married women in the theatre.

As in many other parts of the ancient world the Romans used the image of the phallus to avert magic. Thus the phallus came to be hung around childrens' necks and to adorn the doors of shops and the walls of houses. A phallus was sometimes set above city gates to ward off ill-luck, and under the representation the inscription often appeared, *Hic habitat felicitas*—"happiness dwells here." Such phallic objects exist in most of the museums of Europe, but carefully hidden from public view. In 1834 excavations near Xanten on the Rhine revealed great quantities of phallic amulets, musical instruments with phallic pictures, and many similar objects—all brought to Xanten by the Roman legions, demonstrating without question the ancient preoccupation with phallic phenomena.

Roman ceremonies had to conform to the wishes of the gods. Certain times for marriage rituals, for example, were not thought to be propitious. The whole of May, the first halves of March and June, the Kalends, Nones and Ides of every month, and the numerous Roman festivals were avoided on religious grounds. The best time for a wedding was the second half of June. The wedding rites began on the day before the ceremony: on that day the bride-to-be laid aside the dress she had worn as a child and dedicated it to the gods along with the playthings of her childhood. Particular attention was given to the bride's hair. It was customary to part the bride's hair into six plaits using a lance taken out of the dead body of a gladiator, since such a weapon was held to contain some mysterious power of its own.

The marriage began by taking of auspices early in the morning: the flight of birds was observed with care, or the

entrails of a sacrificial animal were scrutinized. The marriage
guests were solemnly informed of the results of the auspices,
and the ceremony followed, after which the marriage procession escorted the young wife to her husband's house to the
accompaniment of phallic songs and dances. At the house
the husband lifted his bride over the threshold since it would
be a bad omen if she touched it. Consummation itself was
governed by certain sacred customs. The bride prayed to
Juno and to Cincia, the goddess to whom the loosening of
the girdle was consecrated, and the husband loosened the
girdle whereupon the young bride sat down on the phallus
of Mutunus, the god of fertility. Subsequent intercourse took
place in the presence of witnesses and it is likely that the
guests themselves participated. On the following day the
wife, wearing the clothes of a matron for the first time, made
an offering to the Lares and Penates and received presents
from her husband.

As in savage society certain human conditions were
regarded in Rome with special anxiety. We have already
mentioned the attitudes to menstruation and bodily evacua-
tion. Virginity also occasioned various superstitions: virgins
were required, on account of their undefiled state, to officiate
in temples and other sacred places. And at one period in
Italy virgins could not be made to suffer capital punishment.
If a Vestal in Rome was found guilty of an indiscretion
affecting her virgin status, she was taken in solemn procession
to a place near the Colline Gate and entombed alive in a
special underground chamber, along with sufficient food to
last her a few days. She was then regarded as having starved
to death, so that the responsibility for her death did not rest
on the state or prejudice the welfare of its citizens.

There were ways of overcoming the inviolability of secular virgins. One instance concerns Sejanus, a minister of the
Roman Emperor Tiberius, who was convicted of treachery.
The minister and his family were put to death, all except a
virgin daughter who by the laws of the land could not be
executed. Tiberius overcame this impediment by ordering
the girl to be raped by the executioner, and then strangled!

Fear of the unknown or the unusual, that cornerstone of

superstition, made it undesirable in Roman society for deformed persons and other outcast individuals to reproduce their kind. Celsus describes how such men were "infibulated" to prevent them reproducing. The operation consisted of drawing the foreskin forward over the end of the penis and making two holes in it through which a ring was placed and sealed in position.

Preoccupation with phallic phenomena has characterized all ancient civilizations. We have given instances from China, Japan, India, Babylon, Greece, Rome and others. In ancient Britain also, stones and pillars were worshipped as the symbols of the male generative principle. Traces of such worship have been found in many parts of England, Scotland and Wales, though realistic phalli are remarkably rare—in part because the efficient ecclesiastical authorities went to great pains to destroy surviving relics and manuscripts in which such devices were mentioned. Hannay notes that phallic columns were common in Britain and lists many places in which they have been found. Statuettes of Priapus, phallic bronzes, and specimens of pottery covered with erotic pictures have been found wherever there was Roman occupation. For example, in digging the foundations for houses in Moorgate Street, London, a phallus of freestone was unearthed, which served to represent some Roman household god. In the *Archaeologia Adelensis* (1879) Henry Trail Simpson instances cases of rocks on Rombald's Moor, and in other parts of Yorkshire, which he claims are evidence of widespread ancient phallic and serpent-worship. The famous Cerne giant, cut in a hill in Dorset, is equipped with massive genitalia.

Much phallic worship seems to have taken place in Cornwall where use was made of the "holed stones," already referred to in connection with other societies, for purposes of purification. At Lamyon, in the parish of Madron, a large flat slab with a circular aperture was employed: children afflicted with rickets were passed through the hole, symbolizing transit through the female vulva, for the purpose of effecting a cure. Another writer mentions the custom in Selbourne, of passing children in a state of nudity, through a cleft formed by ash-trees, to cure ruptures. In Scotland phallic stones were worshipped as late as the eighteenth century, and in 1935 a figurine of the Earth Mother or Goddess of Fertility was discovered in a neolithic chalk pit at Grimes Graves in Norfolk. Phallic monuments and holed stones have also been found in Ireland and in most parts of continental Europe.

In all societies phallicism, embodying a spectrum of superstitious practice and belief, has been of prime importance. In Aztec religion the virgin was of singular importance in the ritual of killing and resuscitating the maize-goddess Chicomecohuatl. On the selected day the chosen virgin dances along the road in front of the following procession to the sound of trumpets, flutes, horns, and the lamentations and prayers of the crowd. When the music stopped the priest threw the young girl onto a bed of corn cobs and roses and quick as a flash, severed her head from her body. The blood spurting out was gathered in vessels and taken away to fertilize the earth. At the same time the priest skinned the girl and put on the bleeding skin as if it were a tight-fitting costume. Then he danced the same dance among the rejoicing of the watching crowd.

Such ceremonies do not exist in modern America, though superstition necessarily does. One writer,[11] commenting on modern Tepoztlan, notes that men do not expect their wives to have keen sexual appetites: women who *need* men are called *loca* (crazy) and are thought to be in an abnormal condition brought on by black magic. Respectable women express negative attitudes towards sex, and husbands often refrain from arousing their wives sexually since it is assumed that a frigid wife will be more likely to be faithful. Tepoztecans believe that wives who have suffered beatings or other harsh treatment may take revenge through sorcery.

When children misbehave or show an undue interest in sexual matters they may be told that a stranger will carry them off to turn them into soap. Many mothers and grandmothers tell young children stories of owls and coyotes that come out at night to eat bad children, and of bats and opossums that drink blood. In line with Christian tradition children who misbehave are told that they will turn into devils and burn in hell. When children cry they are sometimes told the story of Cahuasohuatun who eats the intestines of such children. Inevitably mutual distrust grows up between parents and children. Children seldom confide in their parents and their questions are discouraged, particularly if the child is asking about sex. The parents will in general give absurd or teasing answers.

Sterility in women is believed to be cause by "cold" in the womb and is treated by massages with warm oil of rosemary and violet. It is also thought that if a child is conceived during the full moon it will be strong: couples often have intercourse during this time for this reason. During pregnancy the midwife strokes the abdomen from right to left, and it is thought that this form of massage will make the birth easier. The pregnant woman must not sleep or rest too much since this would make the birth more difficult. And she should take care not to urinate where an animal has just urinated because the rising steam might cause inflamation of the womb. Nor should she bathe or wash clothes at the stream because *los aires* might endanger the child. Similarly eclipses, rainbows, and earthquakes are all dangerous to an unborn child. Miscarriages are generally blamed on the carelessness of the women.

The mother is discouraged from screaming during the birth because, it is thought, this will cause the child to rise instead of descend: she is given something to bite on and told to keep her mouth shut. When the afterbirth is expelled it is buried under the hearth, since if it is carelessly disposed of or is eaten by a dog the mother may die and the child's face may swell. The dried umbilical cord of a first-born son is thought to be effective cure for certain forms of eye diseases. A new mother is expected to refrain from sexual intercourse for about one year!

Parents questioned in Tepoztlan denied that children were ever involved in any form of sex play though Lewis had little doubt that it took place. During adolescence boys and girls are discouraged from meeting and so they communicate, where literate, by means of letters which may be left in a secret place or delivered by a trusting friend or a child. Widows and girls may deliver love notes, patch quarrels, or entreat some desired girl to become someone's *novia*. Such go-betweens are often disapproved of and suspected of using sorcery to gain their ends. Love magic can be resorted to if courting is not going well. Powdered bone from a human skull, placed in a girl's hand, in her hair, or in a sweet drink, is sure to make her fall in love, and the use of sorcery for revenge by a jilted *novia* is feared by young men. Here, by sticking pins in the boy's image, harm is brought to him by sympathetic magic—thus demonstrating the superstitious continuity from the oldest societies to the present day. Chronic illness in young men is often blamed on some girl's black magic.

Concern at the magic power of women through the potency of virginity, menstrual blood, etc, has often been accompanied by a fear of the female sex organs themselves. One recurrent anxiety is that of the *toothed vagina*. Havelock Ellis has pointed out that there are several remarkable similarities between suckling from the maternal breast and the act of coitus: in both cases detumescence in an organ is observed, which has momentarily swelled and which "through the expulsion of a precious liquid, leads to the complete, physical and psychic satisfaction of both persons involved." Mouth and vagina are even identified in the unconscious, and in delirium the vagina sometimes appears to have teeth: the vagina with teeth has been associated by poets and painters with insectivorous plants such as the "Purple Venus" and has also inspired an instrument of torture, the "Nuremberg Virgin."

According to Freud the fear of the toothed vagina lies at the root of the castration complex: having realized his reprehensible cannibal tendencies while suckling at his mother's breast, the subject fears mutilation from the mother and, when a man, he fears the same from any woman who has replaced his mother in his affections. Similarly the obsession that compels Egaeus, the hero of Poe's tale, to pull out the teeth of the dead Berenice, has been associated with the writer's own impotence. Knowing that he cannot succeed in loving a live woman because he is imprisoned in the memory of his dead mother, he thinks he can liberate himself by taking from the mother—through the simulacrum of Berenice—the weapon which allowed her to destroy his virile powers. At the same time he forces her to undergo a symbolic castration.

It is by means of the vagina that the Eskimo vampire devours her victims.[12] She is so beautiful that men fall fainting when they see her. The young Nukapiartekak can hardly breathe when he sees her but at last manages to approach her in an igloo and to kiss her—

> At first he penetrates into her as far as the knees, then as far as the arms, finally he goes in as far as the armpits. The right arm goes in. Then Nukapiartekak goes in as far as the chin. In the end, with a cry, he disappears completely inside her. When, in the morning, she lights the stone lamp Nukapiartekak is no more. The beautiful woman goes out of the igloo to pass a little water and with her water the skeleton of Nukapiartekak comes out from within her.

In the Marquis de Sade's novel *La Nouvelle Justine*, Lady Clairwil introduces the heart of her lover into her vagina while at the same time kissing his corpse on the mouth.

If men sometimes entertain irrational fears about the castrating capacity of the vagina at other times they deduce, equally irrationally, a woman's sexual capacity by the physical appearance of her genitals. An old example of this is carried in a dialogue between the Yellow Emperor in China and the goddess-instructress. The section, The Forthright Female (Su Nu), is part of the *I-hsing Fang*, a collection of such writings and books compiled by the modern Chinese authority Yeh Te-hui (1864–1927). The Emperor is told that women unsuitable for coitus neglect their pubic hair so that "it resembles an overgrown bush" and that women are unsuited "if the pubic hair is coarse and stiff, like bristles, or if it sprouts wildly and in different directions." Furthermore, "if the lips of the vagina do not cover the Jade Gate, and it hangs below, if the secretions are pungent, then such women are harmful." By contrast in the suitable woman "the outer lips should be high and not hanging, they should be firm without being too fleshy, and the Jade Gate should be so placed that penetration is easy . . . the pubic hair should be smooth and silky, but not profuse. To be without such hair is better than too much, and her Vital Essence should flow at a touch and be sweet-smelling. . . ."[13]

Concern for the physical pleasures of the living is paralleled by similar anxieties about the carnal welfare of the dead. In both ancient society and modern times it has been assumed in many communities that the dead have an active sex-life. With certain nomadic tribes in modern Sweden, for example, it was the custom to put a symbolic female companion in the tomb with a dead man. Reference has also been made to the stone concubines placed in ancient tombs all along the eastern shores of the Mediterranean. The female statuettes have all been manufactured with their feet bound to stop them escaping and it has been suggested that the models have been placed at the disposal of the corpse, ready to satisfy his every lustful desire, and aimed at aiding him over the trauma of death by their pleasingly seductive appearance. Another purpose of the statuettes was thought to be the desire of the local community that the dead should not leave the grave, a particularly unpleasant possibility if the corpse is in a sexually frustrated condition. Up to the time of the Middle Ages it was common belief that the dead would seek carnal union with the living. The Italian Franciscan Ludovici Maria Sinistrari d'Ameno argued against possible doubters—

> There is no lack of individuals so infatuated with their own mischievous knowledge who dare to deny that which has been written by the most authoritative writers and which is demonstrated to us every day, and that is the Demon, incubus or succubus, has carnal intercourse, not only with men and women, but even with animals.

Augustine said "it would be impudent to want to deny

it" and the friar Francesco Maria Guaccio cited eighteen cases, all taken from the accounts of "true and knowing men, whose testimony is above all suspicion," demonstrating how witches and warlocks "calmly practise carnal intercourse with demon incubi and succubi."[14]

Out of the sexual union of living women and demons who had borrowed corpses for the purpose, sons were believed to have been born. A doctor of theology, Maluenda, believed himself to be the fruit of such a union, and many ancient writers—Livy, Plutarch, Pliny, Suetonius, etc—believed in generation in such a manner. Father Sinistrari doubted, however, whether the active semen belonged to the dead man used on such occasions. Nor did he think that the demon had stolen semen from some living man, but settled instead for the hypothesis that "in his commerce with the woman, the incubus Demon generates the human foetus with his own personal semen."

Sexual power can reside, it was widely believed, in the dead—and also in blood. Traditionally, blood has been construed as a sort of super-semen, in the mystical ratio of sixty parts of blood to one drop of semen (hence the "danger" of masturbation). Roman patricians who felt their sexual powers waning used to descend into the arena to drink the blood of beaten gladiators, and in Germany in the nineteenth century epileptics were cured by being given the blood from executed criminals at dawn. The first blood transfusion achieved a temporary cure for Pope Innocent VIII and cost the lives of three youths. Perhaps more bizarre, Erzsebet Bathory found virgin's blood suitable for keeping her skin white. In the Christian communion the magic power of blood is clearly depicted, a ceremony found in similar form in many primitive communities.

Many writers have suggested that blood is an aphrodisiac. The habit of applying leeches to the vagina was widespread in nineteenth century brothels, while in the eighteenth century the medical task of blood-letting offered various pleasures to lovers. The Count of Gernande, a character in de Sade, is delighted to see Justine's blood flow, and in Erich von Stroheim's film *Greed* the dentist kisses his patient when the blood flows from her mouth. In the film *L'Atalante* Juliette will only give way to the hero after a cat has scratched him on the face, drawing blood.

In some ancient beliefs blood was personalized and thought to have an almost independent life, with its own will and caprice. In a similar way, a pregnant woman was sometimes thought to have a devil inside her, and the phallus itself was often assigned an independent volition. An aboriginal tribe in East Africa believed that a disobedient animal inhabited the phallus and directed its actions. A tribe of Indians in Brazil believed that a snake inhabited the penis. In a similar spirit Plato wrote—"the nature of the genital organs is disobedient and self-willed, like a creature that is deaf to reason, and it attempts to dominate all because of its frenzied lusts." Schopenhauer suggested that "the genitals are the real focus of the Will and thus opposite to the brain which represents Idea." And Augustine thought the genitals were named *pudenda* (from Latin *pudere*, to be ashamed) because "they expose the shame of men who although able to control all things to their obedience cannot control these parts." Christian doctrine had it that Satan had fashioned the sex organs, but that the life-generating semen was of divine origin.

CHAPTER FOUR

JUDEO-CHRISTIAN SUPERSTITION

Many Western writers approach the subject of Judeo-Christianity with some trepidation, particularly if they are writing about superstition or mythology. Much in the biblical story resembles acknowledged myth in other traditions. Part of the old Christian tale was that God threw Satan and all his angels out of heaven. Do we believe this any more? Does the Devil even exist? What of miracles and Last Judgement and Second Coming? Does God exist? With such questions unresolved, though debated, in the West it is small wonder that many people are uncertain as to the extent to which Judeo-Christianity may be called *superstitious* or *mythological*.

To the present writer the central tenets of Judaism and Christianity are superstition, unrelieved by making Christianity an established creed, and deriving no rational support from historical incident. A culture or creed is not rendered *non*-superstitious simply because it is part of our own culture: social respectability does not lend truth to irrationalism. In short the author sees the Judeo-Christian philosophy as a vast *superstition,* with irrational consequences in law, education and morality. One moral field in which the irrationalism has been particularly destructive is that of sex.

In its origins the Judeo-Christian tradition exhibited much of the phallic interest evident in other cults: only later did Jewish and Christian philosophers decide to make sex into a problem. The very Ark of the Covenant, the chest of acacia wood housed in the Holy of Holies in the Temple of Solomon, contained amongst other things a sacred stone

G

which, according to certain Talmudic scholars, was a representation of the male and female organs in union.[1] This has been compared with features of the Eleusinian mysteries of ancient Greece which include a rite known as the *arretophoria* named from the Greek words meaning "carrying things not to be mentioned," in which a basket carrying a stone phallus and the "womb" of the goddess Demeter was taken out in sacred procession.

There is abundant evidence in the Old Testament that many gods were worshipped. Joshua told the Israelites that their fathers worshipped other gods (Joshua 14, 2); Abraham appears to have deserted a rival god for the worship of Yahweh (Joshua 14, 3), and afterwards he attempts to introduce the rites connected with the adoration of his old deity. In the words of George Ryley Scott "he continued to worship the phallic principles under the name of Yahweh instead of Baal, erecting pillars, and making human sacrifices."[2] Jeremiah felt obliged to remark: "According to the number of thy cities were thy gods, O Judah, and according to the number of the streets of Jerusalem have ye set up altars to that shameful thing, even altars to burn incense to Baal."

Human sacrifices were offered to Baal-Peor, the phallic god of the Moabites and Midianites, and the priests who superintended these sacrificial rites indulged in cannibalistic orgies. According to Inman, Baal means "My Lord the opener," and Peor signifies "the opening of the maiden's hymen." Thus Baal-Peor claimed from women the sacrifice of their maidenhead. There is evidence for the phallic nature in the Jewish religious system in the reference to the different earths which composed the body of the androgynous Adam, and it has been argued that the revelations of Rabbi Acha (*Gemara Sanhedrin*, Chapter XXX) show that the Jews were acquainted with the mysteries of Eleusis.

The importance of circumcision to the god of the Hebrews strongly suggests a phallic orientation: in Exodus we read how Zipporah threw at the feet of the angry Yahweh the bloody foreskin of her son as a form of appeasement. As with Baal-Peor, Yahweh was referred to as "the opener" (thus "And God remembered Rachel, and God hearkened to her, and opened her womb") and biblical references to Yahweh represented in the form of a bull (the "Bull of Israel") give an indication of his phallic origin. To Scott and others it has seemed obvious that the early Jews—like the Persians and certain Hindu sects—worshipped publicly the male principle, or at least the androgynous (male-predominating) concept.

It is recorded that Joshua worshipped a pillar at Shechem and that Solomon paid homage to a stone at Gibeon (1 Kings 3, 4). In the twenty-eighth chapter of Genesis is the full story of the worship of a pillar by Jacob. These records are significant since many writers have stressed that Yahweh denounced the worship of pillars, despite the fact that even the worship of Yahweh had a strong phallic component. When Moses forbad the erection of fresh pillars he was simply denouncing the worship of pillars representing alien or rival deities. Thus in chapter 12 of Deuteronomy—

Ye shall utterly destroy all the place wherein the nations which ye shall possess served their gods, upon the high mountains, and upon the hills, and under every green tree: and ye shall overthrow their altars, and break their pillars, and burn their groves with fire; and ye shall hew down the graven images of their gods, and destroy the names of them out of that place. Ye shall not do so unto the Lord your God.

That Yahweh himself had no aversion to being symbolized as a pillar, the traditional phallic representation, is clearly shown by the passage in Exodus ("... the cloudy pillar descended, and stood at the door of the tabernacle, and the Lord talked with Moses ... all the people saw the cloudy pillar stand at the tabernacle door: and all the people rose up and worshipped, every man in his tent-door").

Furthermore, Yahweh was everywhere worshipped with the aid of man-like images, some enormous and some small enough to be carried on the person. All the images possessed phalli that were enormous in proportion. It has been suggested that where the word "pillar" is used in the

Old Testament what is actually meant is a priapic statue of unmistakable character. In the sculpture of the Hebrews stress was laid on the importance of the phallic member, until an upright post or stone of any description came to symbolize at once the deity and the phallus. Scott draws our attention to the frequent references to Yahweh as a rock (two examples from more than half-a-dozen will suffice—"Of the rock that begat thee thou art unmindful," Deut. 32, 18, and "The Lord is my Rock," Psalm 18, 2).

Despite the fact that Yahweh incorporated many of the phallic elements current at the time he was not always able to displace the prevailing phallic religions. In Hosea 2, 16 it is clear that on occasions the early Hebrews did not distinguish Baal from Yahweh, and it is evident that Solomon worshipped Baal, Chemosh and Moloch, deities with clear phallic connections.

The upright stone was symbolical of the male god of the Hebrews as well as the male god of the pagans: in the same way, a fissure, an oval or opening came to represent the female principle in nature. It is significant, however, that the Hebrew god was assigned no female consort, as were his pagan equivalents, and Hebrew deity is invariably referred to as male. At the same time a female reproductive element was acknowledged, albeit surreptitiously in the Old Testament as *asherah*, a term deliberately mistranslated as "grove" to disguise the phallicism inherent in the old Hebrew religion. Thus Asherah (the vulva) could be regarded as the female consort of Asher (the phallus).

The deliberate mistranslation, designed for the respectable English Bible, is evidenced by a careful reading of the relevant text. Thus in 1 Kings 14, 15 we read a passage which, as it stands, is literally nonsensical—

> For the Lord shall smite Israel, as a reed is shaken in the water, and he shall root up Israel out of this good land, which he gave to their fathers, and shall scatter them beyond the river, because they have made their groves, provoking the Lord to anger.

Similarly in 2 Kings 17, 9–10—

> And the children of Israel did secretly those things that
> were not right against the Lord their God, and they built
> them high places in all their cities, from the tower of the
> watchmen to the fenced city. And they set them up
> images and groves in every high hill, and under every green
> tree.

Significantly the passage continues, "And there they burnt
incense. . . ." It is hardly likely that Yahweh, capricious a
deity as he may be, would condemn the people for planting
trees!

In many mythologies the image of the ark has served as a
symbol for the womb, and it has been suggested that the
biblical story of the ark is essentially phallic in nature.
Gregory, referring to Noah praying before the body of Adam,
appears to think that Adam represented the primitive phallus,
the one procreator of the human race. One writer[3] has
pointed out that the argo of the Greeks, the Cybium of
Egypt, and the argha (yoni) of India were all represented by
a cup or boat—Osiris standing in a boat, Noah in his ark,
and Iswara, "lord of the boat-shaped vessel," rising from the
yoni, all quite possibly have a common origin, viz. the male
and female elements in clear conjunction ("there would also
now appear good ground for believing that the ark of the
covenant, held so sacred by the Jews, contained nothing
more or less than a phallus, the ark being the type of the
argha or Yoni.") Thus the ark of the Old Testament is intimately related to, for example, the *argha* of Hindu mythology, the Yoni of Parvati, which, like the moon in Zoroast-
rianism, contained the "germs of all things." It may also be
significant that the ark built by Noah sailed on the waters for
a period equal to that of human gestation, namely 284 days,
after which life issued from the ark.

In some mythologies the moon and egg became symbols of
the ark from which they issued when they became parents
of a new race. The ark of Noah symbolized the female
principle with a Lingam, or male principle, for a mast.

According to a Brahman legend it was in this form that the two principles of generation were preserved on the occasion of the universal deluge. At the Dionysia of ancient Greece, an ark or boat, decorated with phallic symbols such as priapi, the navel of the great mother, ripe pomegranates, etc, was carried through the streets.

Another clear sign of the phallicism inherent in old Jewish religion is the prevalence of the phallic oath, disguised through euphemistic translation, in the Old Testament. An old custom for anyone making a vow was to place his hand on his own sexual member or on that of the other party. In the Bible the word *thigh* has often been used for the penis. Thus in Genesis 14, 2—Abraham asks his servant to swear to him: "Put, I pray thee, thy hand under my thigh; and I will make thee swear by the Lord, the God of heaven, and the God of earth." Another instance is concerned with the death of Jacob. With reference to the phallic oath and references to it in Genesis, *Encyclopedia Biblica* (Vol. III, col. 3453) says:

> With regard to the practice of putting the hand under another's thigh, it seems plain that it grew out of the special sacredness attaching to the generative organ; fruitfulness being of specially divine orgin, the organ of it in man could by the primitive Semites be taken as symbolizing the Deity (quoted by Scott, p. 135).

The ancient Egyptians adopted a similar practice; there is a surviving illustration of Osiris taking an oath as he clutches his penis.

Much of what we have said so far about Old Testament sexual interest has been oblique, i.e. the phallic orientation has been inferred. Whether the inferences are sound or not is open to debate, but, in addition, there is much direct evidence to show a biblical interest in sexual activity and moral preoccupation. In fact the Bible, especially the Old Testament, is full of sexual descriptions and a profound concern with what was thought to be sexual immorality.

Sometimes biblical characters, in moments of stress, offer

their daughters to appease hostile crowds. Lot, one of the saints whom God saved from "the cities of the plain," gave his daughters to a mob surrounding his house: "Behold now, I have two daughters which have not known man: let me, I pray you, bring them out unto you, and do ye to them as is good in your eyes...." (Genesis 19, 8). There is a similar sordid tale in Judges (19, 22–30) where a man offers his daughter and another man's concubine to a mob beating on the door of the house: "... so the man took his concubine, and brought her forth unto them; and they knew her, and abused her all the night until the morning: and when the day began to spring they let her go." And as if this wasn't enough for the poor girl, she struggled back to the house and fell down at the door, whereupon the man "took a knife and laid hold on his concubine, and divided her, together with her bones, into twelve pieces, and sent her into all the coasts of Israel."

In addition to taming the mob, biblical women were used to rejuvenate old men. In the First Book of Kings (1, 1–4) it is recorded that David was "old and stricken in years," and that his servants thought a young virgin might improve matters: "Let there be sought for my lord the king a young virgin ... and let her cherish him, and let her lie in thy bosom, that my lord the king may get heat." Alas the technique was of no avail: "... the damsel was very fair, and cherished the king ... but the king knew her not." Some stories in the Old Testament relate to the capture of young women and girls, and their distribution to God's warriors. Thus in Numbers 31, 17 and 18 we read of Moses and his attitude to female prisoners: "kill every woman that hath known man by lying with him. But all the women children, that have not known a man by lying with him, keep alive for yourselves...." An important illustration of the phallic orientation of Old Testament religion comes in a dowry donated by David (1 Samuel 19, 25 and 27): "... The king desireth not any dowry, but an hundred foreskins of the Philistines ... David arose and went ... and slew of the Philistines two hundred men; and David brought their foreskins, and they gave them in full tale to the king, that he might be the king's son-in-law."

Throughout the Bible, particularly the Old Testament, there is preoccupation with sexual events and sexual morality. In Genesis 19, two sisters seduce their drunken father to "preserve his seed" and subsequently find themselves pregnant by him; in Genesis 29, Jacob marries two sisters and takes concubines as well; in Genesis 35, Reuben lies with his father's concubine, and so on and so forth. God even decided to institute a test for unfaithful wives, but not for unfaithful husbands: in Numbers 5, 21, 22 and 27 the use of holy water to detect infidelity is described—"And when he hath made her to drink the water, then it shall come to pass, that, if she be defiled, and have done trespass against her husband, that the water . . . shall . . . become bitter, and her belly shall swell, and her thigh shall rot: and the woman shall be a curse among her people."

There is extensive Old Testament concern with what was thought to be sexual deviation. There are harsh laws about bestiality (Exodus 22, 19, Lev. 18, 23, etc), sodomy (Lev. 18, 22, Romans 1, 26 and 27), incest (Lev. 20, 11–21), rape (Deut. 22, 25–29), fornication (Lev. 19, 20), adultery (Deut. 22, 22), unchastity (Deut. 22, 20 and 11) and castration (Deut. 23, 1). Women are stigmatized as unclean after childbirth (Lev. 12, 1–8) and polygamy is sanctioned (Deut. 21, 15). And in addition to the mischief of Eve, the idea of sin necessarily attending copulation can be found elsewhere (e.g. Psalm 51, 5). In the New Testament Jesus is more tolerant: he refuses to condemn the adultress (John 8, 3–11), but is consistent with one earlier tradition in recommending celibacy (Matthew 19, 10–12): Paul, of course, reinforced the idea (1 Cor. 7) and today few people would sympathize with his severity: "I say therefore to the unmarried and widows, It is good for them if they abide even as I. But if they cannot contain let them marry: for it is better to marry than to burn."

For the early Jews, long before Paul, marriage was a relatively simple affair. As in the persistent Roman Catholic theology the Jews regarded marriage solely as a means to procreation. There was little ceremony and, as in many other parts of the world, the bride was rarely consulted about her intended husband. Often the bride was simply purchased and the only marriage rite was sexual union (see Genesis 24). In the early times no priest was required: the man simply declared "Be thou consecrated to me" and the marriage was complete. Later the words were extended to "Be thou consecrated to me by the law of Moses and Israel." Jews were not permitted to marry women too old or too young to bear children, and if after several years a wife bore no children, the husband was obliged to divorce her and remarry in the hope of better fortunes elsewhere. It was generally assumed that the procreative function was the woman's; thus failure to conceive was never taken to signify inadequacy on the part of the husband. In fact procreation was esteemed so highly that it was illegal to castrate an animal, and to castrate a man was to be a double murderer. And the Jews also laid great emphasis on the importance of premarital virginity—at least on the part of women. If the newly married woman was unable to demonstrate, by the state of her clothes on the morning after, that she married in a pure state then she was stoned to death (see, for example, the sad account in Deut. 22, 13–21).

The Jews were also very worried about masturbation. The Zohar terms it the worst sin of all, and the prohibitions were sometimes carried to extraordinary lengths. It is recorded, for instance, that a Jew must not sleep on his back, wear tight trousers, or touch his penis when urinating, for fear of an involuntary emission. This doctrine can be associated with the stress laid on the significance of procreative activity, and the hostility, in some areas of the Jewish tradition, to methods of contraception for males. The Jews were keen to procreate, and doubly keen to procreate Jews! The orthodox Jew was horrified at the idea of a Jew marrying a gentile, and the early Christians had similar anxieties about Jews. In fact copulation with a Jew was regarded as akin to bestiality and incurred the same penances.

The discernible pattern in Judeo-Christianity, with reference to sexual matters, is one of intimate connection with early fertility and phallic cults, moving gradually to the

exact opposite, an anxious dread of all sexual phenomena.
Yahweh resented the rival deities popular in the early days
of Israel and, to compete, had to incorporate many of their
features: thus the phallic imagery common to parts of the
Old Testament. With Paul and the early Christian Fathers
the anti-sexual trends clearly evident in orthodox Judaism
were reinforced, and Christianity became wedded to a negative sexual philosophy which is one of the most destructive
threads in the whole tradition.

The anti-sexuality inherent in the Judeo-Christian tradition was paralleled by similar elements in pagan philosophy.[4]
Musonius Rufus, for example, argued strongly that no union
of the sexes other than marriage was permissible, and Dio
Chrysostom wanted prostitution to be suppressed by law.
Similar views grew up in the Neo-Platonic and Neo-
Pythagorean philosophies. We are told that Pythagoras inculcated the virtue of chastity so successfully that when ten
of his disciples, being attacked, might have escaped by
crossing a bean-field, they died rather than tread down the
beans, which were thought to have mystic affinity with the
male genital organs. Plato favoured a law to the effect that
"no one shall venture to touch any person of the freeborn
of noble class except his wedded wife, or sow the unconse-
crated and bastard seed among harlots, or in barren and
unnatural lusts." Citizens, he urged, should not be worse
than birds and beasts, which live pure and chaste until the
adult male has paired with the female whereupon they "live
the rest of their lives in holiness and innocence, abiding
firmly in their original compact."

The reasons why Christianity developed such a deep and
surviving hostility to sex can be debated. What is important
is to grasp the extent to which the hostility became
embodied in Western culture and the impact it had on such
specific areas as law, penology, education, and the relations
between the sexes. The first Christian Emperors legislated
to suppress what they thought to be sexual licence, and thus
launched the Christian campaign against sex which is still
being waged today. In instances of seduction, for example,
both the man and the woman, if she consented to the act,

were put to death. Various types of sex criminals in ancient Rome had molten lead poured down their throats. The innocent offspring of illicit sexual intercourse were punished for their parents' sins with ignominy and loss of various civic rights. Some medieval law-books treated bastards on a par with robbers and thieves. Persons of different sex who were not married were forbidden by the Church to kiss each other; and sexual desire itself, even when unaccompanied by any outward act, was regarded as sinful in the unmarried. In consequence anything likely to arouse sexual feeling was condemned: punishments were prescribed by the early Christian Church for the writing or reading of lascivious books, singing wanton songs, dancing suggestive dances, wearing improper clothing, bathing in mixed company, frequenting the theatre, etc.

Underlying the Christian attitude was a disgust at the human body. In St Augustine's much quoted phrase, *inter faeces et urinam nascimur* ("between shit and urine we are born"); St Bernard saw man as "nothing else than fetid sperm, a sack of dung, the food of worms," with woman "the gate of hell;" and Marcion thought it inconceivable that God could be the author of "the disgusting paraphernalia of reproduction and for all the nauseating defilements of the human flesh from birth to final putrescence." And much of this sort of attitude persists in modern men and women with a deeply Christian commitment.

Another indication of the Christian attitude to sex comes to us from the "Articles of War" that must be signed by all Salvation Army soldiers. There we find among other things that "A soldier must not place his hands in a familiar position on any person, or kiss anyone of the opposite sex, other than a relative or that person whom the soldier is courting." Instead of physical pleasure, the Salvationist, faithful to the Christian tradition, is expected to cultivate a spiritual love, to regard man's love of woman (and vice versa) as secondary to the love of God. Often the historic statement of this notion borrowed the language of carnality without shame: thus Origen declared that "the soul ought to adhere to its spouse and hear his word and embrace him and receive the seed of the word from him;" Cassian wrote in the fifth century that chastity is proper to the angels but that man is unable to achieve it without grace; and St John Chrysostom wrote in *Why Women in Orders Ought Not to Cohabit With Men* that God was not only a spouse to virgins but a more ardent lover than a man—

> We admonish you [virgins] that you should make as if to sing a holy song, both at home and abroad, both day and night, both in the streets and in your bed, both with your voice and with your mind, continually uttering and proposing to your soul: Hear, my soul, and see, and incline your ear; forget evil custom and the King shall desire your beauty.

The early Christian prohibition on certain types of dances, clothes, etc, has many echoes in more recent times. In America and elsewhere the police have been known to prohibit certain dances considered "dangerous:" for the same purpose, in Italy in 1926, ten dancing halls were closed at Milan, twenty at Naples, twenty-four at Mantua, twenty at Bologna (in this last incident four hundred teenagers were arrested for dancing). At Mantua twenty-four girls were arrested, promenaded in the town, four in a row, and ten of them were dispatched to a reformatory.[5] In France in 1926, the Mayor of Rocroi prohibited boys under fifteen and girls under eighteen from attending public dances unless accompanied by their parents. Not long ago a decree of the Chief of Police of Long Beach near New York city "forbids couples walking on the beach or bathing to approach each other closer than 6 inches or 15 centimetres; inspectors will be provided with foot rules in order to make sure that bathers shall preserve this distance."

In Spain and Italy in the eighteenth century (according to the memoirs of Casanova), the Inquisition forbade unmarried people to sleep together, and ordered hotel proprietors not to allow the doors of their rooms to be closed, so that inspection would be easier. During the reign of Maria Theresa, the Austrian police were tireless in their efforts to put down the pleasures of sex, and the prison and the cloister were the punishments provided by law. At Brussels, during the Spanish regime, women were not allowed to go for a drive in a carriage if accompanied by a man.

The Roman Catholic Church has always been diligent in attacking the dress of women, from the time of St Bernard, who regarded fashion as a device of the devil, to Pope Pius XI, who declared it to be "deplorable that clothes, the natural purpose of which is to cover a woman's body, should serve the opposite purpose of leading men into temptation." In 1926, in Bologna, a group of over-zealous Boy Scouts took it upon themselves to preserve the Cathedral of San Petronio from profanation by excluding certain female tourists "inadequately" clad: the diligent youngsters came to blows with the husbands of the women! About the same time the Greek dictator Pangalos issued a decree prohibiting the wearing of short skirts, a step copied by a number of modern African states. In 1928 the Hungarian government became so upset by the short skirts on school-girls that it decreed that girls should wear trousers. The clothes taboo does of course have biblical sanctions (1 Timothy, 2, 9): "Let women adorn themselves in modest apparel, with shamefacedness and sobriety. . . ."

In a promulgation of the Bishop of Angers some decades ago specific directives were issued as a guide to "proper" dress. For ceremonies in Church "a high-necked dress should be worn." It should have "long sleeves and should come down well below the knees." Furthermore at marriage ceremonies the bride and bridesmaids should "at most wear a slight décolletage 'à la vierge': they should never have bare arms or cover them merely with a scarf. . . ." At dances, gloves should always be worn (and "no dances which involve close bodily contact should be indulged in"); on the beach "the scanty bathing suit should be discarded in favour of the fuller bathing dresses formerly worn," and girls over ten years of age should wear "long stockings and costumes which cover the knees."

More recently instructions have been given to the guards

outside St Peter's on the question of miniskirts. For many years there have been prominent notices displayed with recommendations on dress for St Peter's pilgrims, but the advent of the miniskirt brought new problems. In August 1969 the Pope's gendarmes met to decide exactly what constituted a too short skirt (one bold captain was reported as saying that "Indecency is in the eyes of a beholder"). The procedure eventually decided upon, in the case of an offending woman, was a courteous salute followed by "We welcome you to the Vatican, miss, but do not feel that your dress at this moment is suitable wear for the interior of a cathedral." On August 23, hundreds of girls were turned away from St Peter's as the anti-miniskirt campaign got under way, and even middle-aged women with dresses two inches above the knee were turned away: however, ragged jeans were allowed under the sacred dome, and some miniskirted girls got through by putting on crumpled raincoats from their rucksacks.

The dress taboo is not confined to Roman Catholics. Luther was so disturbed at the low necklines worn by the girls of Wittenberg that he declared he would never return to that town. In a similar spirit the Council of Trent worried about sexy pictures: "Figures shall not be painted exciting to lust...," and Paul IV commissioned Daniel de Volterra to clothe some of the nudes in Michelangelo's Last Judgement in the Sistine Chapel. Some say that the artist was nicknamed "Panties" in consequence. When Michelangelo's own opinion was sought he remarked that the Pope would do better to work at the reformation of mankind. Clement VIII had intentions to obliterate the entire fresco of the Last Judgement and was only prevented by much argument. Innocent XI was disturbed by the nudity of the baby Jesus and insisted he be provided with a shirt; Innocent XI felt obliged to improve the décolleté of the Virgin Mary; and Pius IX did not rest until the angels supporting pictures of the popes in the Vatican were draped. (The Geneva Bible of 1582 was popularly referred to as the *Breeches Bible* because in it Genesis 3, 7 was so rendered that after the Fall, Adam and Eve clothed themselves in "breeches.")

The early Christians were disturbed at the thought that Jesus would have come into contact with the "parts of shame" during his birth. One idea invented to overcome this deplorable state of affairs was that Jesus exited from Mary in miraculous fashion: one moment he was inside her, the next outside—with no intervening contact with the birth canal or the genitals. Other pious thinkers had it that probably Jesus emerged through the breast or navel (one rebel Ratramnus wrote a long controversial book to prove that Jesus had been born in the normal way). A pressing issue was whether Jesus was divine from the moment of conception or from some later point in his intra-uterine life, and some sort of answer was given on this dilemma in 1856. Some writers, finding it difficult to believe that even God could impregnate the Virgin Mary without her losing her virginity, developed the idea that she was impregnated through the ear by the archangel Gabriel, or by God himself. An Arab physician is reported as saying that "Nafkhae is the name of that particular form of air or vapour which the angel Gabriel is said to have blown or caused to pass from his coat sleeve into the windpipe of Mary, the mother of Jesus, for the purpose of impregnation."[6] In some early paintings the Holy Ghost is seen descending as a dove with the divine sperm in its bill; in other pictures the seminal words are seen passing through a lily, on their way from Gabriel's mouth to Mary's ear, in order to filter out any possible impurities. In one early carving the sperm come direct from God's mouth through a tube which led under her skirts.

Throughout the history of Christianity a superstitious anxiety about and hatred of, sex have persisted. Zinzendorf, an eighteenth century puritanical reformer, taught that there should be no more enjoyment of sex in marriage than of the wine in the sacrament: love should be kept strictly in check, for marriage did not free a man from the restraints of religious discipline. The famous English divine Jeremy Taylor expressed the idea that a husband who loved his wife too much was in danger of an adulterous relationship with her. Thus to make love too often, or too passionately

—even within marriage—is seen as sinful. Puritans would sometimes perform their conjugal duties, doubtless with great loathing, with their wife fully clothed from neck to ankle in a heavy gown, with only a small rent in the appropriate place. No other bodily contact was permitted, so keen were the pious to combat carnality.

The Christian Cathari sect repudiated marriage altogether in favour of a most severe asceticism. Life in the flesh was seen as an imprisonment and propagation as sinful. Sex itself was to be completely eschewed in all its forms. The Cathari aimed to eat nothing connected with the processes of sex: no eggs, cheese, butter, milk, meat, etc.

In the atmosphere of Christian anxiety about sex it was inevitable that even marriage should come to be regarded with some suspicion. Rémy de Gourmont has been quoted: "For the Fathers of the Church there is no middle course between virginity and debauchery; marriage is nothing but a *remedium amoris* which God in His goodness has granted as a concession to human weakness." In the medieval strategy of the Church, marriage could not be performed at certain times of the year: the periods varied but usually included Advent, part of Lent, and the period between Rogation and Trinity Sundays, that is, the greater parts of March, May and December. At one time in the Middle Ages there were only twenty-five weeks in the year when marriages were legal, though a marriage contracted in the forbidden periods, though illicit, was not invalid. Efforts were also made by the ecclesiastical authorities to restrict the hours during which marriage could be undertaken: it was first declared that marriage should take place in daylight, and daylight came to be defined as 8 am to noon. The rule was abolished by the Reformation, later restored, and embodied in statute law in George II's time.

Restrictions on marriage were accompanied by pious restrictions on all sorts of sexual activity, even between married persons. In some of the medieval penitentials fornication was declared a worse sin than murder: even thinking of fornication brought a penance of forty day. Within marriage sexual intercourse was only permitted in one position (*venus observa*, woman on her back with man on top), and married people were obliged to describe, in the confessional, their actual love-making so that the celibate priest could decide upon its propriety. Penalties were prescribed for using variants on the one authorized position: *more canino*, for example, involving rear entry by the male, was viewed with especial horror and a seven-year penance was prescribed.

Not content with such restrictions the Church also struggled to ban sexual activity altogether on certain days and at certain times of the year. Married couples were not allowed to make love on Sundays, Wednesdays and Fridays, which effectively removed the equivalent of five months in the year. Then sexual activity was made illegal for forty days before Easter and forty days before Christmas, and for three days before attending communion (and there were regulations requiring frequent attendance at communion). Sexual intercourse was also banned from the time of conception to forty days after parturition, and of course during any penance.

St Jerome urged members of the early church to refrain from sex on Saturdays and Sundays, the communion days, and saw the purpose of the saint as cutting down "by the axe of Virginity the wood of Marriage." In ancient Welsh law a married priest is seen as belonging among the thirteen things "corrupting the world, and which will ever remain in it; and it can never be delivered of them." Another commentator suggested that married priests were the most subject to malignant demons. Under English ecclesiastical law, laymen were not allowed to have sexual contact with women at "feast-tides and fast-tides." The Scottish Covenanters and the New England Puritans even decided to ban kissing on Sundays, with what success we cannot say. And the Russian household rule, the *Domostroi*, recommends continence on Sunday, Wednesday and Friday, and during the fasts of the Saviour, Lent, and the Mother of God.

Not surprisingly, virginity came to be regarded as a supreme virtue, and saints were seen as particularly saintly if they were able to leave their wives and never return. Many pious souls were sanctified because of their eagerness to

H

desert their spouses. Lecky gives a number of such examples: St Nilus, with two children, was seized with a yearning for asceticism, and his wife was persuaded, after many tears, to consent to a separation; St Ammon, on the night of his marriage, embarked upon a vitriolic criticism of the married state, and his new bride agreed to leave him; St Melania strove to get her husband to agree to her leaving his bed; and St Abraham and St Alexis ran away from their respective wives on the night of their marriage.

The historic hatred of sex has many parallels in the attitudes of the modern Church. In October 1969 the Pope declared to the weekly general audience that the Holy Father is "being subjected, by society, perhaps as never before, to forces of profanity of secularization, and of amorality." Furthermore, society is living under the threat of "extreme eroticism," and the waves of "impassioned sexuality and widespread pornography" must be combated with Christian vigour—

> There are even countries where pornography now is legal. This opens the road to licence, and leads to the abberation of the instinct called [citing references to Freud and Marcuse] the "liberation from conventional scruples." Even some of the most wholesome and reserved areas of society are being salted by eroticism through promiscuity, the pornographic image....

Where a hostility to sex is sustained by a male celibate priesthood a parallel anti-feminist hysteria is sure to develop. Much of the Judeo-Christian hostility to women derives from taboo in primitive society: for example, the neurotic anxiety in early communities about menstrual blood can be found in the Old Testament (Leviticus 15, 19–25)—the sacred nature of blood is emphasized and everything the woman touches is "unclean."

> And if a woman have an issue, and her issue in her flesh be blood, she shall be put apart seven days: and whosoever toucheth her shall be unclean ... and if it be on her

bed, or on anything whereon she sitteth, when he touch-
eth it he shall be unclean ... And if any man lie with her
at all ... he shall be unclean seven days; and all the bed
whereon he lieth shall be unclean. ...

A woman bearing a child is similarly "defiled."

St Paul took up the taboo tradition in being both anti-sex
and anti-feminist. In 1 Timothy 2, 9–12 he urges women to
dress in modest apparel and to remain in perpetual subjection to men—"Let the woman learn in silence with all
subjection. But I suffer not a woman to teach, nor to usurp
authority over the man, but to be in silence." And he adds
by way of justification that "Adam was first formed, then
Eve." In 1 Corinthians the same point is made, and we are
told that man was not created for the woman but the woman
for man.

Paul's "better to marry than to burn" observation, i.e. it
is better to do without sex if you can manage it, but if not
then take a spouse to avoid fornication, became the model for
all sorts of saintly men, united in their anxiety about sex and
their hostility to women. When Paul, in Ephesians 5, declares
that "wives" should be "in subjection unto your husbands,
as unto the Lord," he strives to justify the doctrine thus—
"For the husband is head of the wife, as Christ also is head
of the Church, being himself the saviour of the body. But as
the Church is subject to Christ, so let the wives also be to
their husbands in everything ..." Paul goes on to outline
husbandly responsibilities, but the main theme is clear
enough—women were intended by God to be second-class
citizens and so they should remain.

The early Church Fathers talked of the "tumefaction of the
uterus, and the care of yelling infants," and suggested that
any female should be "filled with shame at the thought she
is a woman." Tertullian, said by some to be the founder of
"Latin Christianity," declared that he "savoured spiritually"
when away from his wife, and wrote to her saying that on
the occasion of the resurrection "there will be more resump-
tion of voluptuous disgrace between us." He hurled his invective at female medical practitioners as well, saying that if a

child was born dead then clearly it was the physician's fault ("If a child is extracted dead it verily was once alive. It is your tubes, your speculums, your dilators and hooks are to blame for causing this destruction").[7]

The Christian hostility to women sometimes reached bizarre proportions. In the sixth century, the bishops attending a synod in Macon (Gaul) earnestly debated whether woman was really a human being at all! In the Middle Ages, the "angelic teacher," Thomas Aquinas, defamed her by depicting her a "failed man" (*mas occasionatus*) and by insisting harshly that she should not be permitted any equality in the Church or in civil society. He spoke about the "use of necessary things, of woman, who is necessary for the continuation of the human race, or of food and drink." Furthermore, "woman was created to help man, but only in procreation ... since, in any other work, man can be helped better by another man than by a woman." We do well to remember the authority of Aquinas in the modern Roman Catholic Church: according to a rescript of Leo XIII in 1879 the philosophy of Thomas Aquinas was to be taught as the only correct one.

Woman was seen by the early Christian Fathers as man's curse. Chrysostom saw woman as an "unavoidable calamity" and Tertullian screams: "Woman! You are the gateway of the devil. You persuaded him whom the devil dared not attack directly. Because of you the Son of God had to die. You should always go dressed in mourning and in rags." The pious writers struggled to heighten the disgust that man can feel for woman. Tertullian reckoned she was *"templum super cloacam"* (*a temple built over a sewer*), and St Ambrose and St Augustine, horrified at woman's genital equipment, were largely responsible for the idea that Jesus never passed down Mary's birth canal but appeared miraculously at the appointed time. St Jerome saw woman as "A tool of Satan and a pathway to hell," and Chrysostom added "a domestic peril, a deadly fascination, and a painted ill." In the Middle Ages one saying had it—"A Good Woman is but like one Ele put in a bag amongst five hundred Snakes, and if a man should have the luck to grope out that one Ele from all the Snakes, yet he hath at best but a wet Ele by the Taile." It was suggested that sexual guilt really pertained to woman since they tempted men, who would otherwise have remained pure. The hostility to women was such that a provincial council in the sixth century prohibited women, on account of their impurity, from receiving the Eucharist into their naked hands. Civil law in the Middle Ages had it that a husband could beat his wife "violently with whips and sticks" or thrash her with a cudgel: iron bars were, however, prohibited.

The theological disgust with women even infected scientific men. Linnaeus in a treatise on nature avoided as "abominable" the study of the female genitals, and the French physician des Laurens asked "How can this divine animal, full of reason and judgement, which we call man, be attracted by those obscene parts of woman, defiled with juices and located shamefully at the lowest part of the trunk?" In modern France, Michel Leiris can write in his *Age d'homme* that he views the feminine organ as "something unclean or as a wound, not less attractive on that account, but dangerous in itself, like everything bloody, mucous, infected."

The Christian hostility to sex and to women inspired one of the most fearsome episodes in European history—the campaign against witches. In about 1260 the Church began actively to punish those engaged in sorcery, but at that time only scorcerers who preached heresy came under attack. By 1451 Pope Nicholas V decreed that sorcerers could be punished even though they were not obvious heretics, and seventeen years later it was decided that sorcery was so serious a crime that the normal legal provisions did not apply. In 1484 Pope Innocent VIII issued the Bull *Summa desiderantes*, at least in part a vicious condemnation of witchcraft. It includes the words

It has come to our ears that members of both sexes do not avoid to have intercourse with demons, incubi and succubi; and that by their sorceries and by their incantations, charms and conjurations, they suffocate, extinguish and cause to perish the births of women, the increase of

animals, the corn of the ground, the grapes of the vine-
yard and the fruit of the trees ... making and procuring
that men and women, flocks and herds and other animals
shall suffer and be tormented both from within and without so that men beget not nor women conceive; and they
impede the conjugal act of men and women.

Innocent drew up this document at the request of two
German members of what Rattray Taylor chooses to call
the "Papal secret police," i.e. the Dominicans. The two men,
Sprenger and Kramer, had been appointed Inquisitors and
began to condemn people for witchcraft in certain German
cities with immense ferocity and clear injustice. Public
opposition to their efforts led to their attempting to gain
papal support, and the bull in question was the result: the
promulgation ends with a declaration that Sprenger and
Kramer have been appointed to investigate the matters in
question, and that they have plenary powers and must be
given every help.

Within twelve months of the issue of the Papal Bull the two
Dominicans prepared the famous handbook on witchcraft,
the *Malleus Malleficarum* (*The Hammer of Witches*), a comprehensive guide for inquisitors. The authors pressured the
Senate of the University of Cologne into endorsing this
odious document. In a few years publication had run to ten
editions, a popularity showing that the work reflected the preoccupations not merely of the authors but of many people in
Northern Europe: the *Malleus* was followed during the next
century by a spate of similar works from other inquisitors,
such as De Lancre, Delrio, Bodin, Terreblanca, and others.
The work has been seen as a treatise of sexual psychopathy,
concerned with three main subjects: impotence, sexual fantasies, and conversion hysterias. Throughout there is immense
preoccupation with sex and fertility.

There is an unmistakable linking in the *Malleus* of female
carnality and the sins of witchcraft. It is highly likely that
the search for witches (nominally sanctioned by Exodus 22,
18, "Thou shalt not suffer a witch to live") represented no
more than the repressed sexuality of a celibate priesthood.

The size of the enormity committed by the Christian Church against women is not always realized. Literally tens of thousands of women in Britain and Europe were burnt to death in the name of piety. In some German villages in the fourteenth and fifteenth centuries scarcely a woman survived, and whole woods were cut down to provide faggots for the pyres. Crazed women under torture named imaginary accomplices in witchcraft, and the holy inquisitors enlisted the civil authority to drag away women from their homes.

The Church's evident hostility to women is clear throughout the *Malleus*. One section carries the heading, *Why is it that women are chiefly addicted to Evil Superstitions?*, and methods of torture are defined in the minutest detail. A recipe for the most extreme forms of sexual sadism could be no clearer. The women are to be stripped, all their hair (including their pubic hair) is to be shaved off, and the tortures (sometimes involving inserting long needles into breasts and genitals) can then proceed systematically—with the attendant priest surveying all the proceedings. For every action the *Malleus* attempts justification:

> ... the hair should be shaved from every part of her body. The reason for this is the same as that for stripping her of her clothes, which we have already mentioned; for in order to preserve their power of silence they are in the habit of hiding some superstitious object in their clothes or in their hair, or even in the most secret parts of their bodies which must not be named.

The portrayal of Woman as witch—as the bringer of disease to man and beast, as the blighter of crops and the cause of impotence and sterility—came as a logical outcome of the persistent anti-feminist posturing and invective of the leading Christian Fathers. The campaign against witchcraft was not an inexplicable aberration of a temporarily-confused Church: it embodied the hatred of women inherent in all historic theology. Woman was the reason for the Fall, and the Fall, leading as it does to the whole theology of redemption and salvation, is at the core of Christian thought.

All the Fathers of the Church proclaimed woman's inferior and evil nature. When Chrysostom wrote that "among all savage beasts none is found so harmful as woman" he was expressing a view that underwrote the bulk of early Christian theology and the ensuing Canon Law that came to influence so heavily the secular legal frameworks of European countries and elsewhere. It is paradoxical that the anti-feminist posturing of the Church should be so much at odds with the attitudes of Jesus. More than one writer has pointed out that Jesus was no misogynist, rather "a feminist to a degree far beyond that of His fellows and followers." He is depicted as a cheerful guest at a wedding; enjoying the company of Martha and Mary; being considerate to the woman taken in adultery; allowing his feet to be bathed in perfume and dried with a woman's hair, etc. There is little in the Gospel image of Jesus to suggest that he would have approved of the policy of his followers in deciding to arrange the systematic degradation of half of the human race. St Paul, of course, has been blamed for the superstitious antipathy that the early Church came to adopt towards women.

The second century was marked by an increasing disparagement of carnal life and specifically of marriage. The Marcionites demanded of all Christians that they be celibate or at least continent within marriage. Satornilus the Gnostic branded marriage and the begetting of children as Satan's work, and Tatian viewed marriage as corruption and fornication. Tertullian attacked female adornment on various grounds, not least that the true Christian is not delighted by the graces that titillate the pagans. The *Acts of Paul and Thecla* praise Thecla's virginity, granting it almost magical powers, and ascribing to apostolic teaching the withdrawal of married couples from the marital relationship. During the reign of Constantine there were eager Christian efforts to exalt virginity and deprecate marriage.

Even female animals were taboo to the Christian monks of certain orders, and to this day Mount Athos is said to harbour only tomcats. Jerome argued that marriage and the saintly life were quite incompatible: after describing the essential triviality of wifely duties he asks "Where amid this is there any room for thought of God?" More than one Christian saint has argued that the only good of marriage is that it produces virgins. Chrysostom noted to his young friend Theodore (who had embarked upon the monastic life only to fall in love with Hermione) that having been affianced to Christ a human marriage would be adultery.

Though priestly celibacy did not become the rule until the eleventh century, even before that time celibate priests were more highly esteemed. In fact, if a priest was married he could only serve at the altar if he refrained from sexual activity with his wife. A tale is told of a priest who kept his wife at a distance: when he was on his death-bed she came to say goodbye, but he forbade her with the words, "Depart, woman, take away the straw, for there is yet fire here."

The superstition that celibacy is superior to the married state, a doctrine first made Christian by Paul, has been enshrined by a vast literature set squarely in the Christian tradition. In *Faith of Our Fathers*, Cardinal Gibbon suggested that Jesus chose his closest disciples on the basis of their virginity, and that when he went to heaven he chose a special band of 140,000 *virgin angels*; the mother of Jesus is represented as a *perpetual* virgin; and Cardinal Gibbon interpreted Matthew 19, 27, to mean that Peter (unfortunately married) "after his vocation did not continue with his wife."

In *Birth Regulation*[8] Stanislas de Lestapis talks of the "true joy of chastity," and in *Family Planning*[9] the same author talks of introducing young people to the "hygiene" of chastity. In the Catholic Truth Society pamphlet, *Birth Control* by G. P. Dwyer, complete sexual abstinence is the "high way of the cross," and in the pamphlet *Why Priests Don't Marry* by the Reverend Edward K. Taylor there is joyful talk of the "beauty of chastity." Pope Pius XI wrote in his encyclical *Ad Catholici Sacerdotii* (on the Catholic Priesthood):

For the Divine Master showed such a high esteem for chastity, and exalted it as something beyond the common power; He Himself was the son of a Virgin Mother, *florem matris virginis*; and was brought up in the virgin family of Joseph and Mary; He showed love for the pure souls such as the two Johns—the Baptist and the Evangelist.

In the Pius XII encyclical *Sacra Virginitas* (Holy Virginity) we are told that sexual sins "are the most shameful and ugliest of human vices." There is also a long theological argument to show the nature of virginity and its superiority over the married state. On p. 6 (Catholic Truth Society publication) we find that "Holy Virginity and absolute chastity pledged to the service of God unquestionably take rank among the priceless values which the Church's Founder bequeathed to the society which He established." And three pages later we discover that the Church received the "essence of her teaching on virginity from the lips of her divine Bridegroom Himself."

One whole section of *Sacra Virginitas* is headed "*Superiority of Virginity*": "holy virginity is more excellent than matrimony;" "The superiority of virginity to marriage ... is ... due to the superior purpose which it envisages;" "The superiority of virginity stands out in still bolder relief if it is considered in terms of its manifold results;" and a subsequent section is headed *Virginity the Angelic Virtue.* It follows from all this that children should be encouraged to live a life of chastity for God:

> We earnestly appeal to fathers and mothers of families to be prepared to offer to God's service those of their children who feel they are called to it. ... Parents should consider what a great honour it is to see their son a priest or their daughter pledging her virginity to the divine Bridegroom.

A bishop of Milan is quoted approvingly—"You have heard O parents—a virgin is a gift from God, her parents' oblation, chastity's priesthood. A virgin is her mother's victim, by the daily sacrifice of which God's anger is appeased."

Pope Paul, eager to emulate earlier papal examples, recently affirmed the Church's historical teaching on celibacy. In an address in October 1969 he prayed to the Virgin

Mary that "she teach us to be chaste with that tremendous and sublime commitment which is our sacred celibacy, a subject much discussed today and not understood by some"— "Celibacy for the priesthood is an everburning flame. It is a superhuman virtue demanding superhuman support." And it is hardly possible to exaggerate the worth of Roman Catholic celibacy: the Reverend Edward K. Taylor writes in *Why Priests Don't Marry* that the successful celibacy of so many men in the service of God "is perhaps the greatest glory of the Catholic Church today."

Celibacy, it may be said, does help the population problem to a degree and some Catholic writers have made much of this. Stanislas de Lestapis notes that complete abstinence is the surest way of limiting birth, and Father Daniel A. Lord tells us that the Catholic Church long ago solved the problem of overpopulation by recommending that large families provide "a generous supply of priests, monks and nuns" who would vow themselves to live chastely, ". . . the fact of their professional chastity kept them from increasing the world's population." Despite all this, however, in July 1969 the Dutch bishops came out in favour of making celibacy optional for priests and suggested changes in the 900-year-old celibacy law. The Bishops argued that the ruling on celibacy is not an untouchable dogma, and that Pope Paul's *Sacerdotalis Celebatus* on the priesthood only made the issue contentious by its uncompromising tone. About one hundred priests in the North of England were given permission to send their ideas on celibacy to Archbishop Dwyer of Birmingham hoping that he would make the views known at the European bishops' conference in Switzerland. In Sydney in October 1969, a former Anglican minister, Peter Rushton, watched by his wife and two of his three children, was ordained as Australia's first married Roman Catholic priest.

As we have noted, the attitude of Jesus to sex seems to have been less neurotic than that of Paul, and he seems even to have preferred the company of prostitutes to scribes and Pharisees: yet in Jesus also are clear signs of the morbid anti-sexuality that came to dominate his church. Jesus said to his disciples,

For there are some eunuchs, which were so born from their mother's womb: and there are some eunuchs that were made eunuchs of men: and there be eunuchs which have made themselves eunuchs for the kingdom of heaven's sake. *He that is able to receive it, let him receive it.* (Matthew 19, 12) (My italics).

This sentiment, taken at face value by Origen and others, is in interesting contradiction to Deuteronomy 23, 1 where we learn that any man "wounded in the stones" or "with his privy member cut off" is not fit to "enter the congregation of the Lord." It is presumably for this reason, with Deuteronomy preferred to Matthew, that the pope's genital equipment had to be checked by a group of worthy cardinals: the pope sat himself in a special chair much like the old birth-stool, and the inspection would commence. If all was well the cardinals would proclaim as they walked past *"Testiculos habet et bene pendentes"* (He has balls and they hang O.K.). There does not seem to be reliable evidence as to when the custom was dropped.

On a number of occasions Jesus urged people to leave their families and to follow him. Since he only called men it is clear that wives would be deserted—"And everyone that hath forsaken houses, or brethren, or sisters, or father, or mother, or wife, or children, or lands, for my name's sake, shall receive an hundredfold, and shall inherit everlasting life" (Matthew 19, 29). And Luke 14, 26 runs along in similar vein—"And if any man come to me, and hate not his father, and mother, and wife, and children, and brethren, and sisters, yea, and his own life also, he cannot be my disciple." Jesus, often portrayed by Christians as a bulwark of the family, was in fact deeply opposed to it where it militated against the fervour of his followers. Wives, children and family must be abandoned in the interests of sanctity—a pious recommendation that was taken up by some of the "saintliest" of men.

One of the clearest superstitions of the Judeo-Christian tradition is that the lives of the saints serve as models for the rest of us. This doctrine is alleged in the context of a general ignorance of what in fact the saints got up to. Some of the best known of the Christian ascetics were those who lived in the Thebaid in Egypt and in the Syrian desert between the third and fifth centuries. They fasted for long periods and lived on a diet of coarse food deliberately prepared in an unappetizing manner: from time to time they would beat themselves with knotted cords and nettles, and some arranged for iron chains to be clamped on their limbs never to be removed; yet others never lay down to sleep, and some stood on one leg for weeks at a time.

One of the most celebrated of these "athletes of God," as they were termed, was Simeon of Antioch (d. 459) known as the Stylite—the "pillar" man—a hermit who lived on top of a high column and who dispensed blessings to pilgrims from afar. The fact that this holy man never washed may have been partly responsible for the remark of the French writer Anatole France (d. 1924) that "Christianity killed the bath," for the only time that the early Church recommended bathing was when it urged the use of a cold bath as a penance. Thus the saint who renounced the world and sex felt obliged to eschew bathing as well.

The harsh regime of the ascetic sometimes led to unwelcome consequences. Jerome tells of the fierce assaults made on him by his own libidinous desires:

> Often when I was living in the desert amid scorpions and wild beasts, I used to fancy myself amid the pleasures of Rome, among bevies of young women. My skin was dry and my frame gaunt from fasting and penance, my body was that of a corpse, yet my mind was aflame with the cravings of desire, and the fire of lust burned in my flesh.

In such circumstances a saint might stand in a tub of cold water, fast to even greater extremes, or beat himself mercilessly with knotted rope.

In his classic work *The History of European Morals,* Lecky relates how, when St Pachomius and St Palaemon were conversing together in the desert, a young monk rushed up to them and with sobs declared that a young woman had seduced him and then vanished in the air: later the young monk committed suicide by jumping into an open furnace. Another monk, in aiding a fainting woman, was unwise enough to touch her: "Passions long slumbering and forgotten rushed with impetuous fury through his veins." He tried to clasp the woman to his heart but "she vanished from his sight, and a chorus of daemons, with peals of laughter, exulted over his fall." Other saints were more successful in avoiding women, imaginary or real. St Basil only spoke with women in extreme necessity, and St John of Lycopolis boasted he had not seen a woman for forty-eight years. A young Roman girl made a pilgrimage to Alexandria to gain the prayers of St Arsenius. When she at length managed to force herself into his presence, begging for prayers and to be remembered, the worthy saint cried indignantly "Remember you! It shall be the prayer of my life that I may forget you!" The Archbishop of Alexandria comforted her by saying that the hermit would pray for her although trying to forget her face "as she belonged to the sex by which daemons commonly tempt saints."

Nechthild of Magdeburg (1210–88) felt herself sick from desperate love for the saviour,[10] and advised "all virgins to follow the most charming of all, the eighteen-year-old Jesus," that he might embrace them. Her *Dialogue Between Love and the Soul* includes such passages as "Tell my beloved that His chamber is prepared, and that I am sick with love for Him" and "Then He took the soul into His divine arms, and placing His fatherly hand on her bosom, He looked into her face and kissed her well." The erotic component in such writing is unmistakable. Margaretha of Ypern (1216–37) managed to conquer her mania for men and then came to believe herself engaged to Jesus. Christine Ebner (1277–1356) embarked upon two years' of masochistic self-torture and imagined she had conceived a child by Jesus after he had embraced her: she cut a cross of skin over the region of her heart and tore it off, demonstrating the linkage between sexual desire and masochism.

St Ammonius tortured his body with a red-hot iron until he was covered with burns, and Christine of St Trond laid herself in a hot oven, fastened herself on a wheel, had herself racked, and hung on the gallows beside a corpse. On one occasion she had herself partly buried in a grave. Fielding noted that she "suffered from obsessions which are now generally recognized as transparent sexual hallucinations." In a number of cases the early Church elevated such practices into a virtue, often canonizing those who practiced them, as in the case of St Margaret Marie Alacoque, St Rose of Lima and St Mary Magdalene dei Pazzi. The Alacoque ingeniously devised new austerities: she sought out rotten fruit and dirty bread to eat, and decided to allow herself no drink from Thursday to Sunday: when she did drink she preferred to use water in which laundry had been washed. Like Christine Ebner she cut the name of Jesus on her chest with a knife, and because the scars did not last long enough, burnt them in with a candle. She was canonized in 1920.

St Rose would only eat a mixture of sheep's gall, bitter herbs and ashes, and the Pazzi is said to have vowed herself to a life of chastity at the age of four. Like St Catherine, she rushed about in a frenzy, calling "Love, Love." After a prolonged rapture in 1585 she had persistent hallucinations of being mauled and pushed about. She would run into the garden, roll on thorns, and then return to the convent to whip herself. On other occasions she would insist that hot wax be dropped onto her skin. The Pazzi made one of her novices stand on her mouth and whip her. She was canonized in 1671.

An underlying superstition common to a number of the historic saints is the notion that dwelling on the idea of dirty and disgusting things, such as spittle or excrement, emphasizes nearness to God. The Alacoque dwelt on these notions with irresistible compulsion. In her diaries she tells how once, when she wished to clear up the vomit of a sick patient, she "could not resist" doing so with her tongue, an action which caused her so much pleasure that she wished she could do the same every day. Mme Guyon, the seventeenth century quietist, describes a similar experience. When St John of the Cross licked out the sores of lepers he described the experience as "pleasurable," and St Rose drank off a bowl of human blood, newly drawn from a diseased patient. When Thomas à Becket lay on his bier in Canterbury Cathedral the vermin that started to crawl out of his cooling body were regarded by the pilgrims as further evidence of his holiness. Macarius went naked into a mosquito-ridden swamp to let himself be stung until unrecognizable; St Simeon ulcerated his flesh with an iron belt; and Evagrius Ponticus spent a winter's night in a fountain so that his flesh froze. . . .

As we may expect, various codes were evolved to oppose sexual behaviour in various forms and the Christian preoccupation came to influence canon and secular law. This, coupled with the enduring anti-feminist posture of historic Christianity, has led to various legal anomalies in the modern world. In the case of adultery, for example, Christianity has generally drawn a distinction between infidelity on the part of a husband and on the part of a wife. Westermarck pointed out that in every Christian land adultery on the part of the wife is a ground for dissolution of the marriage but only in some of such countries is infidelity on the part of the husband a similar ground. In modern times the French code considered it "excusable" if a husband kills his adulterous wife in the act, and such a wife, if not so dispatched could be imprisoned: but the adultery of a husband was only punishable if he kept a concubine in the conjugal domicile, and then the punishment was only a fine. Similarly in the Spanish penal code of 1928 the adultery of a wife is punishable in all circumstances, but that of a husband only if he keeps the woman in the house or if his behaviour gives rise to scandal. And in the Italian code of 1930 the adultery of a wife (*adulterio*) was punishable in all instances, but that of a husband (*concubinatio*) only if he keeps his mistress in his home or keeps her elsewhere "notoriously." In England an Act passed in the middle of the seventeenth century made the adultery of a wife (but not a husband!) punishable by death, but the Act disappeared with the fall of the Commonwealth.

Where the Judeo-Christian tradition has been particularly repressive is in all matters relating to what is considered to be sexual peversion or "unnatual" sexual behaviour. The

Old Testament prescribed death for sexual "crimes" of this sort and the attitude has lingered throughout the tradition. The biblical word sodomite, a translation of *qadesh*, properly denotes a man dedicated to a deity, and so the early Jewish hostility to "sodomites" may have been nothing more than opposition to a rival cult. The sodomites, it appears, were consecrated to the mother of gods, the famous *Dea Syria*, whose priests or devotees they were considered to be. Sodomitic acts were committed with male and female temple prostitutes. In Morocco, for example, it was thought that supernatural benefits could be derived from both hetero-sexual and homosexual intercourse with a holy person.

Paul expressed horror at the behaviour of nations who had "changed the truth of God into a lie, and worshipped and served the creature more than the Creator." In talking of sexual sin Tertullian notes that offenders are banished "not only from the threshold, but from all shelter of the church, because they are not sins, but monstrosities." Basil suggests that sexual aberration deserves the same punishment as murder, idolatry, and witchcraft, and according to a Decree of the Council of Elvira those who use boys to satisfy their lusts are denied communion even after the last hour. The Christian emperors Constantius and Theodosius ruled that sodomites should be punished with death, either by the sword or by burning. Sodomy became one of the four *clamantia peccata* or crying sins. During the Middle Ages heretics were accused of sodomy as a matter of course, and the deep loathing that the act aroused in the church is easily detectable in modern times.

In *Contraception and Holiness* (1964) Leslie Dewart writes that "The moral perfection of the use of these organs requires the congress of man and woman . . ."—thus ruling out such things as masturbation and homosexuality. In the Catholic Truth Society pamphlet *Birth Control*, G. P. Dwyer talks blandly of the "natural repugnance felt by any normal person . . . for unnatural vice between members of the same sex," and this form of activity is cited as a sin "clearly vicious" in itself. Nor are such irrational views confined to Roman Catholics. In 1953, Dr Fisher, the then Archbishop

I

of Canterbury wrote that "homosexual indulgence is a shameful vice and a grievous sin from which deliverance is to be sought by every means," and a year later the Bishop of Rochester commented in similar vein:

> Homosexual practice is always a grievous sin and perversion. Defective sexual intercourse between two persons of the same sex can only be gross indecency under the guise of expressing affection. Even if safeguards can eliminate the corruption of youth, and the practice be confined to inverts of mature age, it would remain the perversion of a wholesome instinct to an unnatural and loathsome end. For all such inverts continence is demanded.

A moderate book on problems of sexuality, written by the Roman Catholic Marc Oraison (a doctor of medicine and theology) was quickly placed on the Catholic *Index of Forbidden Books*, despite the fact that the book was published under the patronage of the Conférence Laenec and with the Imprimatur from Monsignor Brot.

Another type of sexual activity evoking great feeling in the Judeo-Christian tradition is bestiality. It was a Mosaic ruling that in the case of sexual intercourse between a man or woman and a beast, both the human offender and the beast should be put to death (Leviticus, 20, 15). In the Middle Ages, nuns were sometimes accused of it, and, like sodomy, it was made a felonious act by Henry VIII. In medieval penitentials bestiality brought a heavy maximum penalty, from seven to ten years' fasting, according to circumstances. It was thought more sinful to have sexual intercourse with some animals than with others, and an imbecile who used an animal of little value would probably have got off lightly.

The general superstitious doctrine of the sinfulness of sexual activity is enshrined in the Christian penitentials. These pronouncements, intended for the guidance of confessors in estimating the penances to be imposed for an extraordinarily large number of (mainly erotic) sins, were first promulgated in England and came to influence European Christianity in general. The Anglo-Saxon penitentials were soon copied in other lands and were constantly edited and enlarged. The version produced by the Northumbrian historian and theologian Bede (672–735) was one of the most comprehensive.[11]

For a simple fornication Bede ordered a year's fast, and adultery merited a fast of from two to seven years (King Canute reprimanded adulterers by cutting off their noses and ears). Bede was also annoyed at the incidence of masturbation and allocated no less than twenty-five paragraphs to this sin; there were special punishments for masturbation in church, apparently quite common. Fornication with a nun was regarded as incest since nuns were the "sisters" of all mankind; copulation with a nun, quite frequent in some establishments, could also be classed as adultery since the nun was a "bride of Christ." The penitentials were also predictably hostile to people who wrote or read sexy books, sang wantonly, etc; less predictably Bede also came down heavily on people who hung about churches after midnight —since, apparently, the big old buildings were used from time to time for nocturnal orgies.

St Ecgbert, Archbishop of York in the eighth century, composed a set of canonical writings in 729 to rival those of the worthy Bede. Here the poor adulterous bishop is condemned to a fast of twelve years; and if a priest ejaculates semen involuntarily at the sight of a women he is expected to fast for twenty days. If he has a nocturnal emission he must get up at once and sing a psalm. Nocturnal emmissions were a great problem to early clerics. In the sixth century St Augustine II, converter of Southern England and the first Archbishop of Canterbury, inquired of Pope Gregory I whether a priest so "polluted" should be entitled to officiate at mass the following day. The pope decided that if the emission had occured only through natural infirmity—whatever that means—then the priest need only pray and ask God to forgive him. But if the polluted one had consumed too much wine and highly-spiced food the day before, he could only officiate if it were absolutely necessary—and first he must pray, sing psalms, and hand out a few gifts to the deserving poor. Furthermore, if he had been thinking sexy thoughts before going to bed he must in no circumstances conduct mass the following day. Instead he must make a full confession and sing seven psalms with a knee-bend at the end of each verse, followed by a day's fast or thirty psalms with knee-bends.

A husband who has sexual intercourse with a menstruating wife is due for a forty days' fast, nothing compared with the five years ordered for anyone who drinks his own blood or semen. Menstruating women, even nuns, who inadvertently attend divine service must fast for twenty days. If a priest took to habitual fornication he could get a penance of up to ten years, according to circumstance, i.e. number of times intercourse took place, number of different partners, degree of enthusiasm with which he indulged, and the fraud or violence by which an innocent woman was seduced. If a child was born following such priestly misdemeanours the penance could be increased at the discretion of the bishop. A fornicating nun got up to seven years' fasting and laymen who seduced another layman's wife or daughter received a penance of one year, or three if a baby was born. If a bachelor sinned a fast of up to ten years would be imposed, and incest with mother, sister or daughter carried a penance of twelve years.

Fellatio (*qui in os semen effuderit*) earned the practitioner a seven years' fast. If little boys are raped they are punished with a five days' penance; if they co-operated in the assault they earned themselves twenty days. Nor should a man look at his naked wife, and if he proves impotent his wife can at once desert him and seek better luck elsewhere. Conjugal relations on a Sunday, even after dark, were punished by three days' fasting; nor may anyone go to church at any time, after sexual intercourse, without first washing. On and on went the penitentials, growing ever more complex and self-contradictory with every new addition designed to cope with a newly-discovered sexual sin.

Confessors were instructed in later manuals to question penitents closely when they admitted to sexual misdemeanour. It was necessary that the offending person reveal all, so

that the appropriate penance could be imposed. Bishop
Burchard of Worms (d. 1025) gives some examples of such
interrogations in a *Decretum* which also includes the
appropriate penalties for affirmative replies. A typical paragraph runs

> Have you done what certain women are wont to do, con-
> triving a certain engine or mechanical device in the form
> of the male sexual organ, the dimensions being calculated
> to give you pleasure, and binding it to your own or
> another woman's *pudenda*, and have you thus committed
> fornication with another evilly disposed woman or they,
> using the same or other apparatus, with yourself?

If the woman admits such behaviour a five years' fasting
is ordered to apply at all "legitimate Church festivals." Then
he asks inexorably "Have you done what certain women are
wont to do, sitting upon the aforesaid instrument or some
other device of similar construction, and thus committing
fornication upon yourself in solitude?" Admission brings a
one-year fast. If a nun were found to be guilty of such an
offence a much heavier sentence would be given: if she
used "an engine or mechanical device" with a female partner
they were both given a seven-year penance.

The celibacy of monasteries and nunneries sometimes led
to strange results: inmates were visited by lustful phantom
seducers, *incubi* and *succubi*, and nuns were afflicted with
phantom pregnancies, their bellies swelling for months on
end. One amusing tale is told of a lady visited by an unwelcome incubus. She was naturally offended at the efforts of
the demon, and cried out, bringing a crowd of people rush-
ing to her room. Under her bed they found an incubus
hiding, in the likeness of Bishop Sylvanus. In 1329, Pierre
Ricordi, friar of the Order of Our Lady of Mount Carmel
strayed from purity and was imprisoned for seducing three
housewives. Nor were the popes immune from temptation:
Adrian II decided to marry; John VIII was poisoned by the
relatives of a woman he had seduced; Boniface VIII lived
in concubinage with his two nieces and had children by

them; Paul III acknowledged an illegitimate son and a daughter, etc, etc. Of Pope John XII, Wilkes states: "His profaneness and debaucheries exceeded all bounds. He was publicly accused of concubinage, incest and simony." Female pilgrims were afraid to visit Pope John VII because of his licentious reputation, and Bower writes that this pope had turned the Lateran Palace into a brothel and had cohabited with his father's concubine. Women were afraid to visit the tombs of the apostles, since wherever possible he forced married women, widows and virgins to comply with his desires. It is said he died from a blow on the head while in bed with a married woman. Similarly the court of Pope Alexander VI was the scene of unbridled debauchery, according to the unimpeachable papal historian Burchard who tells how, in October 1501, the Pope ordered fifty prostitutes to be sent to his chambers to dance naked before him: the courtesans were ordered to crawl naked on their hands and knees between candle-sticks on the floor, and prizes were produced for those men who, in the opinion of the spectators "should have carnal knowledge of the greatest number of the said prostitutes"—"qui pluries dictos mere-trices carnaliter agnoscerent."

There have been some attempts in history to unite folk religion, with its instinctive acceptance of carnality, with the stern antipathy to sexual matters that has characterized the evolving Christian religion. In one legend[12] the Virgin Mary is even transmuted into a guardian of the fortunes of lovers. The cult of Mary has been compared to that of a Haitian love goddess, Rada Erzulie, worshipped passionately by men but liable to grow jealous if her disciples have sexual relations with human women. Devotion to the Virgin Mary and wor-ship of Erzulie are thus seen as love cults demanding chastity. There has been suggestion that Erzulie rewards her followers by sexual favours in the next world, a compensation that has rarely been associated with Mary.

In Christianity a number of saints have been invoked in matters of love. An obvious example is Valentine, patron of sweethearts. Other saints concerned about amorous matters are Nicholas, patron saint of brides, and St Susan, guardian of chastity. St Winifred, patron of virgins, suffered decapitation rather than marry Prince Caradoc of Wales (various theologians have urged women to commit suicide rather than lose their virginity). A number of male saints have been implored to aid women with their love problems, but such patrons, prepared as they were to tolerate human sexuality, were but a shadow of the phallic equivalents in pagan religion.

Perhaps the most dramatic sexual superstition in modern Christianity is the notion that some singular virtue connects to a refusal to countenance artificial contraception. This doctrine has characterized the whole of Christendom: conscious as many of us are of the extreme statements of the Roman Catholic Church on the subject of birth control, we incline to forget that Anglicans and others were equally fervent (and negative) a relatively short time ago. The unmarried Bishop of London, A. F. Winnington-Ingram (1858–1946) confessed his dismay at the falling birth rate in England and the-then colonies. Birth control he termed "this gigantic evil" and praised the steadfast Roman attitude— ". . . it would ill become the Church of England to condemn less clearly a practice which, if continued, must eat away the heart and drain away the life-blood of our country." And in 1908 a thirty-four member committee of the Lambeth Conference of Bishops, appointed to consider "restriction on population" and other marriage problems, decided to demand the prohibition of "so-called Neo-Malthusian appliances" and the prosecution of all "who publicly and professionally assist preventive methods." Three fundamental resolutions emerged from the conference. The first called upon "all Christian people to discountenance the use of all artificial means of restriction as demoralizing to character and hostile to national welfare;" the second resolution affirmed that "deliberate tampering with nascent life is repugnant to Christian morality;" and the third applauded medical men who had spoke up against artificial methods of birth control.

Repeatedly the Popes—following Augustine and Aquinas —have condemned artificial methods of birth control: Pius

XII, for instance, has declared that even overpopulation "is not a valid reason to spread the illicit practice of birth control." And following papal example some of the Roman Catholic statements have been extreme and offensive to ordinary married people: in 1946, Father Daniel A. Lord classed American wives who used contraceptives with prostitutes and observed that "The advocates of birth control are thorough materialists, to whom a child is just a little animal. . . ." Father Dominic Pruemmer declared that "Birth control is nothing else than mutual masturbation or unnatural lust," and in 1947 Cardinal Spellman declared that education for planned parenthood "assumes that the cure for beastliness is to teach juveniles how to get away with acting like beasts."

In *Family Planning*, S. de Lestapis states that *coitus interruptus* is a form of "trickery," and that where contraceptives are used "there results an emotive psychological dissociation in the woman." This, we are told, is because "It is only in this authentic context [i.e. without contraception], as nature has intended it, that orgasm in the woman has its true sense, that joy and pleasure not only in welcoming her husband but also in assimilating his substance and in being herself transformed by it." Further there is here "all that is needed to encourage the development of frigidity in the woman. . . ." The Reverend Arthur McCormack, in *Overpopulation*, sees birth control as "a sexual perversion, unnatural and sterile," and G. P. Dwyer suggests it can cause sterility, neurosis and other evils. De Lestapis proposes that large families are the answer—"Instead of it seeming strange . . . voluntarily to have a family of five or six children, this way of life should rather be considered as an ideal, an aim to be pursued as far as possible. . . ." This from a celibate priest!

One of the most celebrated papal condemnations of artificial birth control is in *Casti Conubii* by Pius XI. Here we find that artificial birth control is a "shameful and intrinsically vicious" thing. However, the Roman Catholic Church, "standing erect in the midst of the moral ruin which surrounds her," in order to prevent the nuptial union "from being defiled by this foul stain," proclaims that those who use birth control methods are "branded with the guilt of a grave sin."

On July 25, 1968, Pope Paul published the encyclical *Humanae Vitae*—after months of speculation that perhaps at last the Roman Catholic Church would take the opportunity move into the twentieth century. The encyclical restated the traditional teaching and stressed that the rhythm method of birth control was the only one acceptable. The conservatives sighed with relief but many people were greatly disappointed. It was generally conceded that the so-called "safe period" was inadequate as a means of birth control, and even Catholic writers were forced to admit as much: Dwyer—the safe period "does not exist;" Merville O. Vincent—the rhythm method is "frequently ineffective;" and Dr John Marshall, a member of the papal commission on birth control, estimated an overall failure rate of nearly twenty pregnancies for every hundred women. A school teacher wrote in the *Observer* in August 1968 of his four "rhythm" babies, a situation which has led to husband and wife struggling to "stay apart in a physical way"—"we sleep apart, we avoid each other's presence, we stifle the words and gestures of tenderness that could blossom into sexual love. . . ." Such are the fruits of sexual superstition.

CHAPTER FIVE

SUPERSTITION IN SCIENCE

Superstition and silliness have always been a part of science; perhaps not the best part, but clearly indentifiable. For example, there is an interesting feature of certain cuttlefishes, totally misunderstood by early naturalists who should have looked a little closer. The sperm in certain Cephalopoda collect within one of the arms or tentacles, which is then cast off to live for a short time clinging to the female. Cuvier described the cast-off arm as a parasitic worm under the name of Hectocotyle, whereas in fact it should be seen as a primary sexual feature of the species. Early naturalists were also misled by the position of the sex organs in elephants: the breasts, two as in man, lie much further forward than in other quadrupeds, being situated just behind the forelegs; and the female vulva is not situated near the anus as in many animals, but occupies a position corresponding to that of the penis in the male, These circumstances led naturalists to believe that elephants copulate face to face in the conventional human position. It was not until well into the nineteenth century that science confirmed that elephants mate in the position universally adopted by quadrupeds.

Buffon, the great eighteenth century French naturalist, included in a vast compendium of natural history any account that he considered credible. Some of the passages are extraordinary. One deals with the sexual appetites of the higher apes—"Schouten says that the animals which the Indians call orang-outangs are nearly the same height and figure as man ... they are passionately fond of women, who cannot pass through the woods which they inhabit, without

these animals immediately attacking and ravishing them."[1]
Having accepted that these apes rape women on sight,
Buffon adds further details; "Dampier, Froger, and other
travellers, assert, that young girls, about eight or ten years
old, are taken away by these animals, and carried to the tops
of high trees, and that it is very difficult to rescue them."
The testimony of M. de la Brosse, who wrote of his voyage
to Angola in 1738, mentions "that the quimpézes often
attempt to suprise the Negresses, whom, when they succeed,
they detain for the purpose of enjoying, feeding them very
plentifully all the time. . . ." In comparing human beings with
apes Buffon thought it necessary to take into account a
number of factors, including "the vehement desire of male
apes for women, the like conformation of the genitals in
both sexes, the periodic emanations of the females, the com-
pulsive or voluntary intermixture of Negresses with the apes,
the produce of which has been united into both species."

Scientists entertained for many centuries a general confusion as to the nature of generation itself: how did the
business of procreation operate? how did a species ensure
that one generation could yield another? where did new
life come from? The more cautious explorations undertaken
by early scientists were rarely accurate. Aristotle, for instance,
taught that the human foetus developed from a "coagulum"
of menstrual blood, the coagulation being brought about by
the male semen, an idea that persisted for centuries. At
the same time it was thought that animals could be spon-
taneously generated, magically arising from dung and urine.

Harvey, as physician to King Charles, had the privilege of
dissecting the deer in the King's forest.[2] On one occasion he
found in the uterus of a doe, a foetus "the magnitude of a
peasecod . . . complete in all its members," and showed it to
the King and Queen; the "pretty spectacle . . . did swim,
trim and perfect, in such a kinde of white, most transparent and crystalline moysture (as if it had been treasured
up in some most clear glassie receptacle) about the bignesse
of a pigeon's egge, and was invested with its proper coat."
How on earth did the foetus get there? Harvey dismissed
the explanations associated with the name of Aristotle but

two centuries were to pass before scientists were to arrive at the correct explanation. There were two main difficulties: in the first place it was now known that mammals produce eggs; in the second the full authority of the historic naturalists had been used to bolster a whole range of irrationalities. Harvey generalized boldly, in the absence of confirmatory empirical evidence, that all animals come from eggs: the title page of his work on biological generation shows Zeus liberating living beings from the egg, and carries the words: *ex ovo omnia* (all things from the egg). At last the medieval theories of spontaneous generation were on the way out.

Harvey also set about destroying the Aristotelian theory of the coagulum in a series of experiments carried out at Hampton Court and described in 1653. He dissected a newly-mated deer, and showed that, far from there being a coagulated mass in the uterus, there was apparently nothing at all. The people who stood around, including the scientific types, watching the experiment were naturally confused—"But all the King's Physitians persisted stiffly, that it could no waies be, that a conception should go forward unless the male's seed did remain in the womb, and that there should be nothing at all residing in the Uterus after a fruitfull and effectuall Coition. . . ." The King authorized the use of further animals (as what we should now call "controls") to throw light on the subject. A dozen mated does were separated from the bucks; some of the does were dissected by Harvey, and it was found that the uteri contained no seed. The other does fawned at the usual time.

Despite these efforts Harvey still had no idea as to what caused conception. The fact that semen apparently lay dormant for some time before anything developed suggested to him the latency period in the development of many diseases, and he was obliged to fall back on the theory of an "*aura seminalis*," a "kind of contagious property" in the semen—which of course explains nothing. He admitted himself "at a stand" about the precise function of the seed.

At this time semen was regarded as a simple homogenous fluid. Sperm were discovered by Leeuwenhoek in 1676, nineteen years after Harvey's death. The discovery led to all manner of further confusion. What was the purpose of the "infinity of animals like tadpoles" that Leeuwenhoek had revealed within the semen of man and beast? Could they be parasites? Or fertilizing agents? Perhaps they acted as anti-coagulators! Hastily the scientists investigated other bodily fluids such as urine and saliva. Would tiny creatures be found in these also? John Hill declared that the sperm were animals. Buffon decided they were not animals but "living molecules" which increased in number and size after leaving the body. Linnaeus examined sperm and found them to be inert. Some followers of Leeuwenhoek decided there were two types of sperm which copulated and multiplied, and Vallisnieri thought that the function of sperm was to stir up the seminal fluid to stop it coagulating. Du Cerf noted that sperm were few or absent in the seminal discharges of elderly and sterile men.

Spallanzani, an Italian abbé, tried filtering semen and artificially inseminating with it a frog, a tortoise and a bitch —thus proving that sperm were essential to fertilization. At the same time the significance of this did not strike him and he continued to regard the fluid, and not the contained sperm, as the fertilizing agent. Nevertheless Harvey's *aura seminalis* was finally dismissed by such experiments.

Buffon dissected a virgin bitch under the eye of his priest friend, John Needham, and by some extraordinary piece of mismanagement believed he had found spermatozoa in the ovaries. They concluded that ovaries were sperm-making organs. Buffon had also worked out a theory of the origin of life according to which the atmosphere was full of minute living particles, an idea related to the medieval theory of sperm dropping from the stars. To the extent that the air is full of bacteria he was right, but the theory was also intended to explain the mechanism of spontaneous generation. Moreover Buffon thought that the body collected these living particles which then appeared as sperm. In such a fashion was sexual generation accounted for. Cooke elaborated the idea by suggesting that the sperm, if unsuccessful, returned to the atmosphere where they hibernated until required again. In an essay entitled *Lucina sine Concubitu*

(1750), John Hill suggested mockingly to the Royal Society that he had invented a machine for trapping the aerial animalcules:

> After much Exercise of my invention I contrived a wonderful cylindrical, caloptrical, rotundo-concavo-convex Machine (whereof a very exact Print will speedily be published for the Satisfaction of the Curious, designed by Mr H-y-n, and engraved by Mr V-rtu), which, being hermetically sealed at one End, and electrified according to the nicest Laws of Electricity, I erected in a convenient Attitude to the West, as a kind of Trap to intercept the floating Animalcules in that prolific quarter of the Heavens .... when I had caught a sufficient number of these small original unexpanded Minims of Existence, I spread them out carefully like Silkworm's Eggs upon White-paper, and then applying my best Microscope, plainly discerned them to be little Men and Women, exact in all their Lineaments and Limbs, and ready to offer themselves little Candidates for Life, wherever they should happen to be imbibed with Air or Nutriment, and conveyed down into the Vessels of Generation.

The work of Marcello Malpighi, the "father of embryology," gave rise to one of the most protracted controversies of the eighteenth century. Malpighi decided that the development of the embryo was a simple unfolding of what was already there, the view known as preformationism. Today we know that this interpretation is erroneous, that in fact a uniform material differentiates to form the various organs.

The doctrine of preformation had certain theological implications: if in the first egg there was implicit all subsequent eggs then original sin could be explained and the curse on Adam and Eve justified. The microscopist Swammerdam, finding a perfectly formed butterfly within a chrysalis, adopted the idea, as did Malebranche. In 1684, Zypaeus claimed to have seen minute embryos in unfertilized eggs, and De Graaf's supposed discovery of the mammalian egg—when in fact he was looking at blastocysts, or large cells from which the microscopic eggs develop—seemed to confirm the idea. When sperm were discovered scientists immediately looked there for the origin of the embryo, expecting to find some sperm with tiny arms and legs! Soon it was widely thought that complete miniature human beings, termed "homunculi," could be detected among the newly-discovered spermatozoa. Leeuwenhoek himself denied being able to see them, though he supported the preformationist theory. More successful, the colour-printer Gauthier d'Agoty claimed to have seen a miniature donkey, cock and horse in the seed of the appropriate animals. Dalenpetius' claim to have seen a homunculus take off its coat was intended as a joke.

The discovery of sperm split the preformationists into those who thought that the preformed adult was contained in the egg, and those who believed that the new human being was enshrined in the sperm. In 1805, Good wrote that "Every naturalist and indeed every man who pretended to the smallest portion of medical science, was convinced that his children were no more related, in point of actual generation, to his own wife, than they were to his neighbours." By 1768 to doubt preformationism was gross impiety. Charles Bonnet made the specific claim that within the first female of every species were contained the germs of all subsequent offspring, each generation within the previous one. This doctrine, known as encapsulation or emboîtment, entailed the proposition that when the last "Chinese box" had been opened there would be no more germs to develop, and the human race would cease to be. Bonnet, as fervent Catholic, raised the doctrine to the rank of dogma and claimed it as "a triumph of the sensual over the rational imagination." Bonnet did useful work on aphids and other small creatures, but his scientific writings tend to be interspersed with effusions about angels—which tends to cloud the issue.

The preformationists, keen to speculate imaginatively about embryos, were less eager to examine them, holding that more could be learned from the adult. In 1759, the twenty-one year old Caspar Friedrich Wolff published observations which eventually led to a more accurate interpretation of the nature of sexual generation. Having studied plant embryos and the development of chicks, he dedicated a doctoral thesis to the great preformationist von Haller, who paid little attention. Wolff also drew absurd comparisons between the vessels in a plant and an animal's arteries, and in general relied too heavily on speculative adventures uninformed by adequate empirical data.

Francesco Redi, the seventeenth-century Italian naturalist and poet, was puzzled by how flies got into cherries. The idea of spontaneous generation was well entrenched and it seemed quite plausible that flies were generated by urine or decaying matter of various sorts: van Helmont and others thought that veal engendered flies.

Redi took a snake, some fish, and a slice of veal and placed them in four sealed jars, with similar samples in open jars: the first batch of material did not decay, and the second did. Redi concluded bravely that "the flesh of dead animals cannot engender works unless the eggs of the living be deposited therein." Nevertheless, despite this insight, he was still disturbed to find cherry flies emerging from cherries and insects from plant galls. He studied the problem for the rest of his life, but without solving the mystery. Three years after his death, in 1700, Vallisnieri showed how the larvae originate from eggs already deposited in the plants.

In 1748, Needham, in collaboration with Buffon, repeated Redi's experiment in a more refined manner, but with the intention of proving the doctrine of spontaneous generation. He boiled mutton broth and put it in a sealed jar. After a few days the flask was opened and was found to be swarming with multitudes of organisms. The experiment was repeated with other animal and vegetable matter, with identical results. Spontaneous generation, it was concluded, had been proved.

The situation was made even more complicated by Bonnet's discovery of parthenogenesis. Taking a newly-born aphis, Bonnet watched it almost unceasingly for twelve days as it passed through its moults: at 7.30 am on 1 June 1740 he saw a young one born from it. At the same time Trembley's work on hydra (which generate offspring simply by budding) showed that not all reproduction was from eggs. Trembley drew the first picture of cell division ever made, and has been dubbed by some the "father of experimental zoology."

It was as late as 1827 that Karl Ernst von Baer announced his discovery of the genuine mammalian egg, 159 years after de Graaf had believed himself to have made the discovery: von Baer remarked;

> Led by curiosity I opened one of the follicles and took up the minute object on the point of my knife, finding that I could see it very distinctly and that it was surrounded by mucus. When I placed it under the microscope I was utterly astonished, for I saw an ovule just as I had already seen them in the tubes, and so clearly that a blind man could hardly deny it.

Even at this stage—with Leeuwenhoek having discovered sperm, and von Baer the mammalian egg—the scientists of the day were unable to take the step of imagining sperm fertilizing eggs. And this despite such clear pointers as half-cast children and hybrids in other species. In fact another fifty years had to elapse before the crucial fact was established that a single sperm fertilizes an egg. And at last the idea of spontaneous generation was abandoned. In all, two hundred years elapsed from the discovery of spermatozoa to the first rudimentary understanding of fertilization, and many mysteries still remain—why can only one sperm enter an egg? by precisely what mechanism does the successful sperm reach the vicinity of the ovum? how does the fertilized egg come to differentiate into all the bodily organs? and so on and so forth.

Scientific errors and confusions about sexual topics have been rife. From the time of the Greeks (when sex was thought to be determined by which testicle supplied the semen) to the twentieth century irrationality and self-contradiction has abounded. As we have seen, some of the great names in biology have been associated with utterly mistaken doc-

K

trines. Even Darwin does not escape; he believed, for example, in pangenesis (the doctrine that the embryo contains contributions from all the organs). A sketch by Leonardo da Vinci (reproduced in *Science Journal*, June 1970, p.81) is anatomically correct except for one detail, a direct connection is shown between the uterus and the breast, as in the fifteenth century was believed to exist. (The real connection between the two has only recently been understood and concerns the hormone oxytocin released by the brain in response to stimulation of the breast or the vagina.) In a recent (1938) *Encyclopedia of Sex Practice*[3] we read the extraordinary suggestion that Japanese illustrations of coital positions rarely show the woman lying on her back as "the genitals of the women of the yellow races lie farther back than those of European women," thus demanding different modes of sexual union. Further the Oriental woman "has another interesting anatomical peculiarity," this being that "many Chinese and Japanese, including physicians, have no knowledge of the existence of such a thing as a hymen." And this is perhaps due to the fact "that it is not particularly well developed in the women of the yellow races."

In medieval China, court physicians were sometimes worried that attendant eunuchs might grow a second penis, an anatomical impossibility but an idea taken quite seriously at the time.[4] The belief led to more than one ruler ordering that court eunuchs be "trimmed" from time to time to ensure that no second organ could develop. One such tale features a certain Chief Eunuch Wei. Rivalry grew between him and the Chief Minister, whereupon the offended minister hit upon the idea of informing the Emperor that the organs of his eunuchs were sprouting again and that the eunuchs had designs on the royal concubines. The Emperor, Ch'ien Lung, hastily ordered an inspection and put the Chief Minister in charge: the consequence was that the eunuchs, including Wei, had to submit to further punitive surgery.

The production of eunuchs meant that in medieval China and elsewhere there was a supply of male organs available to scientists and surgeons working in that field. Sometimes eunuchs begged physicians to transplant organs back again, with results that are not hard to imagine. Criminals and prisoners-of-war also suffered castration and helped to swell the organ "banks."

In the seventeenth-century work, *Jou-pu-t'uan*, Li Yu describes a penis graft in detail. One of the characters in this tale is made to remark, "I have seen your advertisements in which you claim to increase the size of a small member. Perhaps you will kindly explain how this miracle is performed and whether you can guarantee one of giant proportions." The Master of Medicine, to whom the enquiry is addressed, replies that it all depends upon the original material. "First on its dimensions, secondly on what size you want it to be. Then there's a third consideration—will you be able to adapt yourself to the drastic change?" Asked for further explanations the Master of Medicine continues:

> I trust you will be able to follow the language of a medical explanation; to begin with, do you need simply a couple of inches on the end? If so, I can give you an ointment that will bring about this magical change without difficulty. First it makes the implement insensitive to heat and cold and temporarily stops the need to urinate. In this state it is then "washed," "smoked" and "pulled." Please excuse these professional terms. The "washing" is for enlarging, the "smoking" for toughening and the "pulling" for lengthening.

This treatment, which may seem a rather obvious, if unreliable, method of increasing the size of the penis, by no means exhausts the capacities of the talented Master of Medicine. More ambitiously, if the "really diminutive Male Peak" has to be drastically enlarged, it may be necessary to restructure the vessels, sinews, skin and flesh; "But such surgery is only recommended to those who feel that the chance to have a super-size implement outweighs all other considerations of life." The patient must have the "purpose and courage to face the prolonged treatment." The treatment consists of using sections of the erect penis of a dog to supplement the penis of the patient:

I wait until the mounted dog is about to ejaculate . . . . then take out my surgeon's knife and slice it away with a single cut. As it is lodged in the bitch, I then carefully carve it out of her . . . In a matter of moments, I first cut lengthwise down the enlarged penis, quartering it into long segments. Then the patient's member, after being anaesthetized, receives four incisions. Into each of these long cuts I slot a slice of the dog's member—the flesh must still be warm—rub the assembled strips with a special healing ointment, and then bind the lot in tight with bandages. With luck, there will be a perfect grafting of man and dog.

After about three months "the new implement can be pressed into service," by which time, when erect it is twenty times the size of a normal organ.

The Chinese man has been seen by some as a "boy-man," with narrow shoulders, a minimum of body hair except for the pubic region, and hands that were often soft like those of a woman. In such circumstances the Chinese male may have had doubts about his masculinity. C. N. Frazier and H. C. Li in their *Race Variations to Syphilis* (1948) quote the findings of an examination of one hundred skulls at Peking Medical College: evidence is adduced to the effect that "the Chinese male resembles the White female more than he does the male of the White race."

One of the first "standard works" on sexuality was the *Geneanthropeia* of Giovanni Sinibaldi. This remarkable work is, in the words of Alex Comfort,[5] "the fount and origin of very nearly all the major nonsense about reproduction, inheritance and sexual matters generally which was to haunt counselling literature to the present day." Sinibaldi was born at Lionessa and became professor of medicine at Rome. The book, which first appeared in 1642, is dedicated to Cardinal d'Este: by 1658 it arrived in England in a bowdlerized popular version as *Rare Verities, the Cabinet of Venus Unlock'd . . . Printed for P. Briggs at the Dolphin in St Pauls Church-yard.*

In Sinibaldi there is a mix of careful observation and clear superstition. Witchcraft and astrology are not excluded and there is more than a dash of Roman moral theology. The *Geneanthropeia* in fact represents a compilation of sexual folklore as accepted by the medical profession of the day. Sometimes questions are asked and answers attempted. "What are the physiogonomical signs of Lust?" "What are the signs of Virginity?" "Why do night pollutions afford more pleasure and do more debilitate than a man's spontaneous copulation with a woman?" The answers are not always what one might expect: "A little straight forehead denotes an unbridled appetite in lust." "Little ears demonstrate aptness to venery." And "It is an infallible sign of this, if a man is bald and not old; but if old and not bald, you may conclude he hath lost one of his stones or both." It is also claimed that a sad or weeping woman cannot conceive, and that the same disability attends too much passion —"Experience tells us that Virgins ravished are never with child; or, on the other side, if she be possest with too much joy." And with a rather different emphasis to that encouraged by our Chinese Master of Medicine, Sinibaldi offers advice on "How to shorten the Yard, being too long."

He also wondered whether spirits mate. And could nature have dispensed with coitus altogether, so that we could reproduce by what Samuel Butler called a harmless form of vegetation? What sort of sex life did Adam and Eve have, and did the Blessed Virgin have a menstrual cycle? Was not nature rather remiss in only providing man with one sex organ.

Sinibaldi saw homosexuals not as sick or simply different, but as morally repugnant, and he urged the lash and the dungeon are the best possible treatment for their condition. A variety of symptoms and signs accompany an appetite for sex—hunch back, red nose, elephantiasis, piles, frequent emission, constipation, gout, etc. All coital positions other than *Venus observa* (woman on her back with man on top) are not merely sinful but physiologically harmful. Impotence can arise from diseases of the reproductive system (fair enough!) or from witchcraft (!), or from wanting the desired object too much. Cold feet are also a great impediment to successful sexual performance. The best aphrodisiacs are rest, boredom, sleep, red meat and woman, followed by wine and prosperity, fun, music and pleasant surroundings. As far as sexual experience with boys is concerned—"this excitative to lust being forbidden, I choose to pass over it in silence . . . wherefore the holy fathers are forbidden, familiarity with women, boys, and heretics." It is also noted that flogging gets some people going—"Dear God, what have we here? A prodigy? That pleasure should come from pain, sweet from bitter, lust from bloody wounds? Does the same road lead to torment and to delight?"

There were also certain medical effects of coitus to be noted, and Sinibaldi classifies these appropriately into indications and contra-indications. Firstly, sex is good medicine for many conditions, e.g. for the phlegm, for certain types of epileptics, especially those affected in childhood (who commonly lose their fits about the age when sex starts to interest them), depressives and other mental patients, "from greensick virgins to the furious." Sex can also be a useful cosmetic—"there are some who by temperament or through the ravages of disease have a skin as rough as wood or as hard as marble. There is nothing better to restore the normal consistency of the flesh in such, than moderate use of sex. . . ." And Sinibaldi is not averse to citing personal experience: he knew "a young man who was squat, hard, bristly and rough, so that his arms looked like oak branches. He married, and in a few months he was a man of flesh. This he frankly put down to his wife, avowing that the use of her bed had turned him from wood to flesh."

Sex does, however, have a certain number of disadvantages or "contra-indications." Various behaviour disorders, Sinibaldi believed, can be caused by lust and sexual addiction. For a start the sexual act is exhausting: athletes in training on a concentrated diet can be allowed a little sex, but soldiers are unfitted for battle if allowed to indulge—which is why Moses gave a day's leave after a nocturnal emission. Sex also dries up the "natural balsamic quality" and shortens life, and as a corollary whitens the hair and makes it fall out, especially if one picks an old partner.

Needless to say, menstruation is magical—as it always has been in human society, and coitus with a menstruating woman is fraught with all sorts of unpleasant possibilities. Sex is also dangerous, Sinibaldi tells us, after a hot bath, but not after a cold one. And intemperance in sex can lead to elephantiasis and blindness. If one wishes to retain a soprano voice then sex should be avoided. Avicenna, who influenced Sinibaldi, informs us that sexual excess leads to pins and needles, weak legs, coldness, yellowness, backache, insomnia, bad breath, gooseflesh and swollen gums. Sanctorius is quoted approvingly as he lists eleven mischiefs effected by sexual excess. If a person has been moderate in carnal matters then there are clear signs to detect—"the signs that coition has done no ill are these: a urine evenly concocted as it was before, an agility of body, easier respiration, and no loss of weight."

Sinibaldi also had a view, odd to modern ears, that the foreskin is the seat of male sexual pleasure and adds greatly to enjoyment in the female. Why should this be so? "I ask my reader not to treat this question as trifling or ridiculous, for the Jewish women, Turkesses and Mauritaniae, their husbands being shorn, make much of it, and most gladly accept the embraces of Christians (so it is said)."

The sources used in the *Geneanthropeia* are Aristotle, Rhazes, Avicenna, and such immediate predecessors and contemporaries as Rondelet and Paulo Zacchia, "my very good friend." Sinibaldi aimed at producing what was in part a handbook of sex hygiene, and it came to represent a substantial portion of medical philosophy in such matters. Even well into the nineteenth and twentieth centuries medical men reiterated, for example, Zacchia's description of coital postures in which some are described as "weakening" or unfavourable to fertility.

In the eighteenth century, medical opinions on sex were a mixture of superstition and quackery. A certain Dr Graham, a friend of the more sober John Hunter ran a Temple of Health, in which Emma Hamilton appeared through a trap to sell bottles of his balsam, and couples could hire a Celestial Bed for purposes of procreation. Around the same time

Ebenezer Sibly, MD FRHS, invented the Solar Tincture for Men and the Lunar Tincture for Women. He also wrote about the green sickness of young virgins—"If such are the effects of the seminal fluid when reabsorbed by the male, how powerful must it be when suddenly mingled . . . with the circulating fluids of the attracting female!" The *ancient virgin*, we are told, deprived of this "animating effluvia" tends to infirmity, ill temper and disease. And it is well known that lack of coital experience at a time "when nature seems to require it, lays the foundation of many disorders in females. . . ." Here is what happens if, young woman, you hold back from sex:

> . . . the prolific tinctures seize upon the stomach and viscera, obstruct and vitiate the catamenia, choke and clog the perspiration vessels, whereby the venal, arterial, and nervous fluids become stagnant; and a leucophlegmatia, or white flabby dropsical tumour, pervades the whole body, and quickly devotes the unhappy patient to the arms of death.

If "venereal embraces" are not at hand Sibly does provide a means of mitigating the worst aspects of sexual deprivation. We are urged to consult page 217 of his *Family Physician* which suggests leaves of mugwort, briony, and pennyroyal infused for four days in two quarts of soft water; the Lunar Tincture is added to the solution, and the patient is told to imbibe a gill-glass, three parts full, three times a day. The medicine has a variety of beneficial effects—". . . it unclogs the genital tubes, purges and cools the uterus and vagina, promotes the menstrual discharge, cleanses the urinary passages, dissolves viscid humours in the blood, sharpens the appetite, stimulates the nerves, and invigorates the spirits. . . ."

At the same time, as in all societies, the use of aphrodisiacs was widespread and often enjoyed the support of the best medical opinion of the day. Even in early societies the use of love-potions and such like was not encouraged only by sorcerers and mystical herbalists: the scientists of the day played their part, and lent a type of authority to what folk tradition had already enshrined. In medieval China, for instance, court physicians would recommend a number of solutions to lost potency, a favourite being the consumption of fresh human brains. Senior eunuchs seeking regeneration were sometimes in the position of being able to order the execution of the emperor's enemies and common criminals: the eunuchs would order that a few heads be split open and the contents brought to them while still warm. And the time-honoured potions, based on human liver, placenta, semen, menstrual blood, etc, were still in widespread use. These were claimed to be good for strengthening the *tsing* (semen), for "restoring the Male Peak," and for curing convulsions. In his *Collection of Fine Cures* (twelfth century), Wu Khiu stresses the remarkable restorative powers of the human placenta ("No distinction should be made between the Purple River-Boat (placenta) of male or female children, though that of the first child is particularly beneficial"), and suggests that after a final cleansing of evil spirts it should be dipped in a bowl of mother's milk.

Another Chinese physician of the twelfth century, Tung P'in, recommended cooking the placenta in alcohol, then kneading it, and then serving it as "dumplings" with certain herbs and powders. In the fourteenth-century *Medical Treatise* of Li Shi-Chen the *tsing* is described as the Flame and Fire of the Soul, and it is suggested that the distress of eunuchs was because the Vital Essence never found release. And Li recommended a potion for the eunuchs. "The semen of virile young men should be mixed with the excrement of hawks or eagles and taken in pellet form."

As early as the sixth century BC, Susruta, one of the medical authorities of India, recommended the eating of animal testicles as a cure for impotence. Pliny urged that men anxious about their virility eat the testicles of a horse, or the right testicle of an ass, pulverized and mixed with wine. To stimulate desire in their womenfolk, the men of the Arunta tribe in Australia fed them with the testicles of the opossum or the kangaroo. Paracelsus, following the Greeks, taught that nature made orchids in the shape of testicles as a gentle hint that the juice of the plant will "restore his lewdness to a man."

In 1776, Dr Théophile de Bordeu, physician to Louis XV, suggested that the essentials of masculinity are determined by a secretion of the testicles which passes into the blood. Arnold Adolf Berthold, a German professor of physiology, proved the theory in 1849 by castrating four roosters and implanting one testicle each into the abdominal cavities of two of the four capons: the untreated capons became fat and lethargic, whereas the ones with grafted testicles began chasing hens again.

It was not long before men of science thought that such experiments had implications for human potency and vigour. When Dr Charles Edouard Brown-Séquard, the famous French physiologist, reached the age of seventy-two in 1889, he decided to take steps to restore his lost youth. He mashed testicles of dogs and guinea pigs in a salt solution and injected a sample into himself. For a while he thought himself a new and younger man.

In the nineteen-twenties, bogus rejuvenation experiments were attempted by Dr Eugen Steinach in Vienna and Dr George Voronoff in Paris. Steinach cut the *vas deferens*, the duct leading from the testicle, on the theory that the cells producing a sex hormone would then be stimulated to renewed activity. After they had undergone the operation a number of elderly men boasted, for a short time, of their recovered youth. On one occasion a man of seventy-two, scheduled to give a lecture in London entitled "How I Was Made Twenty Years Younger by Eugen Steinach," was found dead in bed on the morning before the lecture. With the aim of restoring lost potency, Dr Voronoff performed a number of "monkey-gland" operations, involving transplanting testicles from chimpanzees to men. The monkey tissue was soon destroyed in the new human evironment.

Learned doctors in the Middle Ages and through the Renaissance produced numerous dissertations on love potions. The records of the University of Basel contain a medical disputation of 1622 in which it is argued, against much folk belief, that menstrual blood is not effective in love potions.

On the other hand, the authoritative *Medicus Microcosmus* of Daniel Beckler, published in Rostock in 1622, in Leyden in 1633, and in London in 1660, declared positively that efficient philters can be prepared from human blood. Some doctors, conscious of their duty to patients who may have been tricked into taking love philters, looked for means of countering their effects. J. H. Moliter, a professor of philosophy and medicine at Jena, urged in 1676 the use of mineral baths containing alum, antimony, arsenic, nitre, salt, sulphur, and vitriol as an infallible cure for the victims of philters. Johann Hartman, professor of chemistry at the University of Marburg in the seventeenth century, urged emetics, holy water, and antimony taken internally.

A seventh-century Greek physician, Paul of Aegina, suggested a diet of aphrodisiac foods, obscene books, and ointments containing the root of narcissus with the seeds of nettle or anise, as a cure for impotence. In 1563 a man was reported to have cured his impotence by anointing himself with the bile of a raven in oil, and *The Chemical Analysis of Ants* (1689), written in Wittenberg by S. B. Manilius, referred to the use of ants in an aphrodisiac ointment.

In the nineteenth century a wide range of aphrodisiacs were being manufactured in various countries. In Cincinnati, Ohio, in 1858, Dr William A. Raphael claimed that his Cordial Invigorant, at three dollars a bottle, could make possible the "wonderful prolongation of the attributes of manhood." Dr Raphael explained that the formula was his own improvement on one given him by an Arab sheik who, at the age of one hundred and nine, had fathered seventy-seven children, the youngest only one week old. "The cordial stimulates the sluggish animal's powers to healthy action, and with vigour comes *natural desire*. It brings the system up to the virile point and *keeps it there*."

In the early part of the twentieth century the Interstate Remedy Company in the US advertised a "Recipe that Cures Weak Men" in the *Baptist Record* and *National Police Gazette* simultaneously. In 1913 a reporter for the Chicago *Tribune* noted a variety of products in a drugstore window —"Knoxit, sure cure, one to five days," "Make-Man Tablets,"

"Zip," "Aphro Tonic Rejuvenator," and "Passionettes, six boxes for $5." By 1928 the American Medical Association was busy closing the mails to Hercules Vitality Tablets, advertised with the words "Be a Healthy, Robust Man" and "Be an Attractive Woman." The tablets were found on analysis to contain iron carbonate, calcium carbonate, dandelions and strychnine.

The U.S. federal authorities investigated in 1918 a gland extract placed on the market, Orchis Extract, "the Greatest Known Treatment for Weak Men." The origin of the extract was suggested by a picture of the Chicago stock yards on advertising booklets, and it was stated in the company literature that the extract was made from the testicles of rams.[6]

Following Steinach and Voronoff, Dr John R. Brinkley collected over twelve million dollars in twenty years for transplanting goat glands into sixteen thousand men, and for selling by mail his Special Gland Emulsion. He began his work modestly in 1913 with an advertisement in the Greenville (South Carolina) *Daily News*, "Are You a Manly Man Full of Vigour?". Readers who had doubts about their manliness could have an injection of coloured distilled water into hip or arm for only twenty-five dollars. In 1917 Dr Brinkley, in the back room of a country store, transplanted goat testicles into the scrotum of a farmer who complained of having "no pep." The following year the farmer's wife had a son. Soon after this the hard-working doctor had acquired a hospital and a radio station at Milford, Kansas. He raised a flock of Toggenberg goats, which had the advantage of being practically odourless in comparison with Angora goats, and each patient was permitted to choose his own goat. Three times Brinkley was a candidate for the office of governor in Kansas. Eventually the Federal Radio Commission closed his radio station, and Kansas revoked his medical licence.

In the nineteen-sixties various aphrodisiac products were still being advertised, including one received by Gifford from, of all places, Greenville, South Carolina: this capsule contained testosterone, yohimbine, and strychnine. A large company recently advertised to the medical profession a combination of male and female sex hormones, calcium and vitamins. There was mention of declining metabolic function and degenerative changes of the ageing: two attractive young women looked off to the right of the picture as one said to the other, "It's hard to believe that he's sixty."

The famous Dutch gynaecologist, Dr Theodoor Hendrik van de Velde (1873–1937), in his book *Ideal Marriage*, holds that yohimbine is a genuine aphrodisiac, but too dangerous a drug for general use. However, in a sexual emergency requiring special efforts to please a "beloved partner," he would expect proper foods to achieve the required result. Meat is recommended, particularly venison, and eggs also are a sexual stimulant, a restorative after sexual exertion, and a producer of sperm cells. The virtues are cited of beets, carrots, turnips, celery, artichokes, asparagus, and crayfish soup.

Nor did Van de Velde stop at food and drugs as an aid to sexual arousal. Hot cushions or hot pillows applied to the small of the back were said to be often "surprisingly helpful." This is akin to the suggestion of Dr Marie Stopes, author of *Married Love,* who shocked the world in 1918 by proclaiming that sex could be fun, on the subject of beds. To get the best out of sex, and to aid procreation, the marriage bed should be placed in a north-south direction "in tune with magnetic currents." Gifford quotes the reaction of a woman from Northern India to this proposal—"What nonsense, every Hindu knows that the bed should be placed in an east-west position."

Marie Stopes also had odd ideas about the behaviour of the body during sexual intercourse, teaching that a complete sexual climax involved the seizure of the tip of the penis by the cervix uteri of the female, resulting in exquisite pleasure and immediate fertilization. In fact there are no muscles or nerves available to perform such a feat. This error follows similar confusion in Mrs Annie Besant whose *Law of Population* had reached its hundred and tenth thousand by 1887. She too called on non-existent muscles and nerves to perform formidable feats:

The complete ignorance of their own bodies, which is supposed to be a necessary part of "female modesty," makes necessary a preliminary word on the mechanism of the womb and the process of fertilization . . . the womb may be regarded as a bag with its mouth kept shut by an india-rubber ring. . . . This mouth opens slightly from time to time during sexual excitement and this makes it possible for spermatozoa to work their way in . . . the opening under excitement is very slight.

And both Dr Stopes and Mrs Besant believed that a perfect climax for both sexes makes fertilization more likely.

Menstruation was another phenomenon about which medical science entertained odd attitudes. In the nineteenth century a French physician, Dr Avrard of La Rochelle, spoke of the "excretory function of menstruation" and suggested that menstruation was a way of "ending a congestion." Most doctors at the time were firmly committed to the idea that menstruation and ovulation were totally unrelated. In 1878 the *Lancet* carried an article by a prominent medical man suggesting that menstruation was caused by the more rapid rate of growth found in female children as compared with males.

The *British Medical Journal* (1878) carried a correspondence debate on the subject of menstruation. One person asked if others had information about the tendency of hams to rot, when prepared by a menstruating woman. A physician replied by saying that hams did indeed rot, but only when the pig was female and was menstruating at the time of its slaughter.

Difficulties during the menopause have been attributed by serious scientific writers to dancing, immodest dress and contraception. Thus in 1902 Emma A. Drake of Boston wrote in her *What a Woman of Forty-Five Ought to Know:*

. . . women who as young girls have been negligent of care at the menstrual period; who have danced, or exercised excessively in other ways without regard to this time, though they may or may not, as a consequence, have suffered at the periods thereafter, yet at the menopause they will be quite likely to pay the debt of abused nature, by sufferings which bear at least some proportion to their negligence . . . The "slaughter of the innocents," which today has reached such huge proportions all over our land, in the prevention of conception or the production of abortion when conception has taken place, is another large factor which contributes to the discomfort and disease of the women who lend their hand and heart to this soul-destroying business. . . .

For the last three hundred years the subject of masturbation has also been surrounded by "scientific" and other superstitions.

In 1708 Boerhaave was writing that "the rash expenditure of semen brings on a lassitude, a feebleness, a weakening of motion, fits, wasting, dryness, fevers, aching of the cerebral membranes, obscuring of the sense and above all the eyes, a decay of the spinal chord, a fatuity, and other like evils." Boerhaave quotes a number of medical authorities in support of his contentions: a Dr Baynard is invoked, and "a certain author" who remarks with enthusiasm "if we turn our eyes on licentious Masturbators we shall find them with meagre Jaws, and pale Looks, with feeble Hams and legs without Calves, their generative faculties weaken'd if not destroyed in the prime of their Years; a Jest to others and a Torment to themselves." Thus the masturbator must go in terror of being uncovered by zealous compatriots who know the signs, and must also face the horrors of gonorrhoea, stranguries, priapisms, impotence, blindness—and damnation.

A Roman Catholic in 1758 published in Lausanne a book called *Onanism; a treatise on the disorders produced by masturbation* which was quickly translated into many languages.

Tissot argues, in line with many of his clerical colleagues, that *all sexual activity is harmful,* by reason of the rush of blood to the brain which it causes, starving the nerves, making them more susceptible to damage, and thereby inducing insanity. Solitary orgasm is most dangerous of all: it can be practised so conveniently and at such a young age that excess is inevitable; moreover the enormity of the crime itself brings immense dangers to the individual. The masturbator, in addition to the minor condition of being perpetually exhausted, is also liable to melancholy, fits, blindness, catalepsy, impotence, indigestion, idiocy and paralysis.

Rush wrote in the first American textbook of psychiatry (1812) that "this solitary vice" (i.e. masturbation) has consequences more serious by far than "the morbid effects of intemperance with women:" masturbation, we are told, leads to "seminal weakness, impotence, dysury, tabes dorsalis, pulmonary consumption, dyspepsia, dimness of sight, vertigo, epilepsy, hypochondriasis, loss of memory, fatuity and death." After such a catalogue of misfortune death would seem almost a blessing! Esquirol (1816), a French medical authority, commented that masturbation "is recognized in all countries as a common cause of insanity," and some years later he reckoned it responsible for suicide, melancholia and epilepsy.[7] German writers soon added blindness, skin diseases and other ills to the long list of troubles that the masturbator might expect.

By 1839 Sir William Ellis, superintendent of Hanwell Asylum, was writing that "by far the most frequent cause of fatuity is debility of the brain . . . in consequence of the pernicious habit of masturbation." By 1852 it was generally conceded in England that "the habit of the solitary vice" gives rise to hysteria, asthma, epilepsy, melancholia, mania, suicide, dementia and general paralysis of the insane. W. Griesinger in his *Mental Pathology and Therapeutics* (1867) states that "onanism is an important and frequent cause of insanity, as of all other physical and moral degradation," and in 1895 Henry Maudsley could write that masturbation "notably gives rise to a particular and disagreeable form of insanity characterized by intense self-feeling and conceit."

From 1850 to 1879 a variety of anti-masturbation surgical measures became increasingly popular, and by 1880 any neurotic parent who wanted to tie, chain, infibulate, encase in plaster (leather or rubber), beat, frighten, castrate his sexually active children could find respectable medical authority to justify his action. Some medical experts even recommended cauterization of the genitals and clitoridectomy. Dr Sylvanus Stall tells the male offender what he can expect: nothing less than a strait-jacket or having their hands tied with ropes to iron rings in the wall ("And I am sorry to say that even these extreme measures are not always successful in restraining them or effecting a cure!"). As early as 1786 S. G. Vogel had recommended in his *Unterricht für Eltern* putting a silver wire through a boy's foreskin to prevent masturbation, and in the nineteenth century adults were counselled to adopt the "common practice" of sleeping with the hands tied. J. L. Milton of the Hospital for Diseases of the Skin suggested that a chastity belt be used. Spiked or toothed rings were devised to fit round the penis. And a paper by Yellowlees suggests that infibulation (use of the silver wire) was widespread ("I was struck by the conscience-stricken way in which they submitted to the operation on their penises. I mean to try it on a large scale, and go on wiring all masturbators ...") If a recalcitrant mental patient tore out the ring he should thereafter be kept tied up.

A certain John Moodie, who described himself as "MD and Surgeon," invented a device to prevent female masturbation and to render seduction less likely:

The Moodie girdle of chastity consisted of a cushion made out of rubber or some other soft material ... This cushion or pad formed the base into which was fixed a kind of grating, and this part of the apparatus rested upon the vulva, the pad being large enough to press upon the mons veneris ... The bars of the grating ... were so arranged in the pad that when in position they pressed up against the labia majora opposite the vagina. The whole apparatus was affixed by belts to a pair of tight-fitting drawers and secured by a padlock, a secret flap being made so as to close over the key hole. ...

In a French surgical instrument catalogue (1904) chastity belts for both sexes are illustrated as stock, and similar equipment is shown in an English catalogue for 1930. Not

L

long ago "gloves, wire, to prevent onanism" figured in English catalogues with chains for lunatics as standard mental hospital equipment.

In the middle of the nineteenth century Dr Isaac Baker Brown, later president of the Medical Society of London, introduced the operation of clitoridectomy to prevent the epilepsy, hysteria, convulsive disorders of all sorts supposedly caused by masturbation: both children and adults were operated upon in his specially instituted London Surgical Home; in 1866 he published details of forty-eight such cases. In 1894 Dr Eyer of the St John's hospital, Ohio, decided to deal with nervousness and masturbation in a young girl by cauterizing the clitoris; this failing, a surgeon was brought in to bury the offending organ with silver wire sutures, which the child then tore to resume the habit. The complete organ was then cut out (this horrific case is reported by Eyer as "Clitoridectomy for the Cure of Certain Cases of Masturbation in Young Girls," *International Medical Magazine*, 3, pp. 259–262, 1894–95). In 1897 a Texan had his penis forcibly amputated to prevent further masturbation!

One of the keenest upholders of sexual superstition in the nineteenth century was William Acton, a specialist in diseases of the urinary and genital systems who worked first in Paris and then in London. He first came into the public eye through his writings on prostitution. His best known work, however, is *The Function and Disorders of the Reproductive Organs*, which went through six editions between 1857 and 1875. Acton himself remarks in the book that his opinions were much sought after by educators and parsons, by general practitioners, and by people of the upper middle class in London whose sex lives were giving them trouble.[8]

For a start it is highly significant that the book is entirely about men and male sexuality. Apart from two short passages not a word is said about women. Acton's failure to appreciate that perhaps something should be said about female genitals in a book talking generally about "the Reproductive Organs" leads Marcus to suggest that the world of the book is "part fantasy, part nightmare, part hallucination, and part madhouse." In the opening pages of this celebrated work Acton pleads that working-class young men should be lectured on the merits of fatigue as a means of reducing sexual desire, and that cultivated parents should not allow their children to read the classics. Desire and inflamed imagination lead to loss of semen, whether in sexual intercourse or not, and loss of semen inevitably meant loss of vigour, health and ultimately sanity. ("My own opinion is that taking hard-working intellectual married men residing in London as the type, sexual congress had better not take place more frequently than once in seven or ten days.") At the same time Acton suggests that intercourse twice on the same night might enable "the patient" to restrain his feelings for as much as a fortnight thereafter ("This, however, is only a guide for strong healthy men.")

Much of Acton's concern is that man's *vital substance* should not be squandered. Wet dreams, he thinks, can be avoided by will power, and by eschewing soft mattresses and drinking after eight. During the day one's thoughts and actions should be carefully controlled. An enema of cold water or opium before retiring is not a bad idea. Acton himself tried passing an instrument up the rectum to press on the vesiculae, and thus mechanically inhibit the emissions, but he found that too much local irritation resulted. It was more successful to cauterize the urethra with silver nitrate. And the company of sexy females should be avoided at all costs ("I need hardly add the obvious advice that he should above all things leave off any acquaintance he may have formed with immodest women"), as should stimulating literature ("strict injunctions should be given to abstain from the perusal of any work containing allusion to the subject of his complaint, or any work which would be likely to produce erotic ideas.")

Sexual activity among children, the early interest in genitals and subsequent sex-play, was known to Acton, and he predictably disapproved. The causes of such deplorable behaviour included hereditary predisposition, "irritation of the rectum arising from worms," bed-wetting, irritation of the "glans penis arising from the collection of secretion under the prepuce," and, in boys who do suffer from such irritation, manipulation of the penis while washing it in order to reduce the original stimulus. The foreskin is seen as morally objectionable since "it affords an additional surface for the excitation of the reflex action. . . ." He adds in a footnote—"In the unmarried it additionally excites the sexual desires, which it is our object to repress."

Acton urged married men to sleep with their hands tied together to prevent the dangers of yielding to temptation in weak moments.

If loss of semen, voluntarily or involuntarily, was one problem to men of scientific bent, so was its effective control to prevent conception. In this area also, superstition and absurdity have been rife. Hippocratic writers suggested that semen should be "shaken out with bodily movement," and that fat people are less fertile than thin ones (people who wanted to avoid pregnancy should put on weight).[9] Lucretius also proposed that diet be controlled as relevant to fertility, and suggested that sterility was caused by "thickness" or "thinness" of semen, a quality effected by certain types of food. Pliny the Elder suggested the wearing of worms taken from the body of a hairy spider as a means of preventing conception. Discorides recommended the fruit of the "Chaste tree," and willow leaves to cause "inconception." Asparagus worn as an amulet could make a person sterile.

Avicenna, following Soranos, reckoned that partners should avoid reaching a climax at the same time if they wished to avoid conception. Soranos thought that menstrual blood and a woman's "seed" were one and the same thing, and so believed that conception was most likely when sexual intercourse took place close to the time of menstruation.

The sixteenth century expert, Culpeper, who took the pseudonym "Aristotle," produced *Aristotle's Book of Problems* which deals with various aspects of reproduction. Whores, he tells us, are never pregnant because "diverse seeds corrupt and spoil the instruments of conception for it makes them so slippery that they cannot retain seed, or else 'tis because one man's seed destroys another." And the reason why twins are born is strictly according to Galen, i.e. the several receptacles in the womb are the cause—the trio of uterine horns on the right side engender boys, and the left, girls. The seventh horn is the source of hermaphrodites. He decides also that "if a woman should have more than seven children at once, it should be rather miraculous than natural."

In the seventeenth century women were bled to remove sterility. However, Culpeper advised against bleeding girls before puberty as he thought this caused barrenness. And another author, quoted by Wood and Suitters, had reservations about the practice of bleeding men—"But amongst other causes of barrenness in men, this also is one that maketh them barren, and of the nature of eunuchs, the incision, of cutting of their veins behind their ears, which for a disease many times is done."

Various writers were concerned at maximizing the chances of conception. Culpeper advised the husband against withdrawing too quickly after sexual intercourse, as this made it possible for "cold to strike into the womb," a most dangerous occurrence. If a woman was keen to conceive she should rest on her right side, and avoid sneezing, coughing or making any violent movement. Nor should intercourse be too frequent—"grass seldom grows on a path that is commonly trodden."

A number of eighteenth-century writers about venereal disease recognized that the sheath offered some protection. Daniel Turner remarked in 1717 that the condom is the best preservative "our libertines have found out at present." But some men condemned it as blunting sensation and often chose to "risk a clap, rather than engage 'with spears thus sheathed'." Some condemned such forms of birth control. Joseph Cam, for instance, thought it wicked to tell men to "use *machinery* and fight in *armour*."

The great medical authority Girtanner observed that condoms reduce pleasure "and annihilate the natural end of cohabitation;" nor do they ensure immunity since the least hole will permit contagion and in any case the membrane may tear. He castigated the negligence of the police, "who do not seek to prevent the sale of an invention so shameful and so detrimental to repopulation. . . ."

It was also widely believed in medical circles that water

could have a fecundating effect of its own or at any rate serve
as a medium for sperm transport. Averroes told a tale of a
woman who conceived in a bath "by attracting the sperm
. . . of a man admitted to bath in some vicinity unto her."
Sir Thomas Browne, commenting in 1646 on such cases,
observed "Tis a new and unseconded way to fornicate at a
distance . . .," but clearly had doubts that such things could
happen. Other commentators were more credulous, however,
and stories circulated of women being made pregnant by
bathing in water used by a man or by caressing a female
friend who had just had sexual relations with her husband.

In the eighteenth century also a clergyman produced a
best-seller, postulating an aerial origin for spermatozoa. A
contemporary suggested that "the whole extent of the air
. . . is full of the seeds of everything that can live on earth"
—theories that we have noted in connection with Buffon's
research in the process of reproduction. Such ideas were
often supported by respectable medical men.

In 1879, Dr C. H. F. Routh wrote an introduction for the
reprint of a paper he had given at Bath the previous year
before the Obstetrical Section of the British Medical Association. The paper dealt with current contraceptive practices
—a subject of legitimate medical interest, one may think.
Routh, however, went to some length to explain how he
came to write on the subject ("It was desired by some distinguished members of the profession to open the discussion,
so as to offer them a public opportunity of condemning,
with no uncertain sound, baneful practices which they knew
had been making their way into this country.") The "indecor-
ous" subject is *Onan's crime*—"coverings are used by the
males, plugs and injections by the females to complete their
shame." And to allude to such vile practices (withdrawal,
condoms, occlusive pessaries, etc) is, in Routh's words,
"almost defilement." Of intra-uterine devices Routh observes
that their insertion requires the assistance of a person of
some skill, and he asks the momentous question with all
moral weight—*Who put them there?* Such was the neurotic
state of much medical opinion in the nineteenth century.

In American textbooks of the mid-nineteenth century the

medical profession was largely hostile to all forms of contraception. *Coitus interruptus* was viewed as mere masturbation; *coitus reservatus* carried various dangers with it; condoms inflamed the vagina, etc, etc. In 1875 the Cornell University authorities found it necessary to remove a chapter on the control of conception from a popular book written by one of the faculty professors. And parallel with such nervous reticence on the part of medical men a whole host of bizarre contraceptive remedies were being proposed, some by quacks, some by respected medical authorities, and some by people with no medical knowledge. . . .[10]

Infanticide was mentioned by William Godwin in a reply to Malthus (1801), as an expedient practised in China but repulsive to Englishmen. Godwin himself comments that "if the alternative were complete, I had rather such a child should perish in the first hour of its existence, than that a man should spend seventy years of life in a state of misery and vice." By 1838, infanticide was proposed as a serious way of limiting population by an author calling himself Marcus in two booklets: *On the Possibility of Limiting Populousness* and *An Essay on Populousness*.

Marcus suggested killing all babies after the third born into every poor family: and of the third children, three out of four, chosen by lot, were to be killed at birth. These children were to be put to death by mixing a deadly gas with the air they were breathing, whereupon the infants so killed were to be buried in beautiful colonnades, adorned with flowers, closed and gently warmed in winter, resorted to by all classes as places of recreation.

In 1806 Thomas Ewell, MD, a surgeon in the US Navy, suggested that "A remedy of corrective or fruitful nature might be found by embracing only in vessels filled with carbonic acid or azotic gas." Convinced that oxygen was necessary for conception he explained that "coition will always be unfruitful unless it be done in pure air, so that some oxygen gas many be protruded before the penis into the uterus." Thus the chances of conception must be greatest early in the night, for "the air of beds before morning is well known to become so foul as to extinguish burning tapers." At the same time how could the high fertility of Negroes be explained, except by their habit of copulating by day, "exposed to the sun, on the sides of hills, where the air is uncommonly pure?"

Karl August Weinhold (1782–1829), professor of surgery and medicine at the University of Halle, suggested the compulsory infibulation of poor bachelors between the ages of fourteen and thirty, as well as of beggars, unemployed and chronic invalids on relief, domestic servants, journeymen and apprentices—until they were capable of supporting a wife and children. Infibulation, Weinhold held, was as easy as vaccination: the foreskin is drawn up and four or five inches of lead wire are pushed through it, to be soldered together and stamped with a metal seal so that no-one might remove and replace a ring without discovery. Tampering with the ring between the ages of fourteen and seventeen should be punished by flagellation; from eighteen to twenty-four by the treadmill; and from twenty-five to thirty by a starvation diet of bread and water.

As far as can be ascertained the ideas of Ewell and Weinhold led to no practical results. On the other hand, John Humphrey Noyes (1811–1886) ran a religious community where a method of "male continence" was daily practised, with a certain degree of contraceptive success. A man would put his penis into the woman's vagina for anything up to an hour and a quarter, avoiding sexual climax, eventually to withdraw in a detumescent state after the woman had experienced orgasm once or several times. The man did not ejaculate during the procedure or after withdrawal; nor, it was claimed, did he feel the impulse to do so.

In his *Bible Argument; Defining the Relations of the Sexes in the Kingdom of Heaven* (1848), Noyes suggested that the separation of the amative from the propagative put sexual intercourse on the same footing as other ordinary forms of intercourse such as conversation and shaking hands. Sexual intercourse with male orgasm, but without any procreative intention, was akin to masturbation: the habit of making intercourse a quiet affair was natural, healthy, favourable to amativeness ("it *vastly* increases . . . pleasure"), and effective in controlling conception.

The idea of "male continence" also featured prominently in the writings of Dr Alice Bunker Stockham (1833–1912). In place of all conventional methods of contraception she recommended "sedular absorption" (*sedular*—pertaining to seed), involving intercourse "without culmination." Such an approach, requiring days of *thoughtful preparation* as *a course of training*, was claimed to provide "the highest possible enjoyment, no loss of vitality, and perfect control of the fecundating power." During the hour-long act, visions of a transcendent life might be experienced with consciousness of new powers.

Once a woman has conceived, coitus (many medical authorities have believed) is most ill-advised. Hippocrates opposed it (together with hill-climbing, washing, and sitting on soft cushions). Galen was against coitus during lactation, since intercourse was thought likely to spoil the taste of the milk and rob it of important ingredients. In his *What a Young Husband Ought to Know* (1900), Sylvanus Stall cites authorities to show the hazards of sexual intercourse with a pregnant woman: "Coition during pregnancy is one of the ways in which the predisposition is made for that terrible disease in children, epilepsy . . ." (Dr J. R. Black); "Indulgence during pregnancy is followed by the worst results of any form of marital excess . . . the results upon the child are especially disastrous . . ." (Dr J. H. Kellogg).

In more modern times a number of physicians have warned against intercourse towards the end of pregnancy for fear of infection. Dr Masters and Mrs Johnson have seen this as "a residual of the preantibiotic days." There is no more danger of vaginal or cervical infection late in pregnancy than at any other time. And should it occur it can be dealt with as it would be earlier in pregnancy.

Another area of sexual superstition relating to women is that associated with sexual climax or orgasm. There is a view, associated originally with Sigmund Freud, that women can experience two sorts of orgasm: one in the vagina and one focussed on the clitoris. The debate on these two supposed types of sexual experience (which is to be preferred? how are they both evoked? do they both in fact exist?) has occupied much of the psychoanalytic, psychological and physiological literature. The informed view at the moment, with weighty evidence to back it, seems to be that the vaginal orgasm is a myth, that sexual climax in the woman can only be realized through involvement of the clitoris.

Theodoor Hendrik van de Velde (1873–1937), the Dutch gynaecologist already mentioned, was a keen proponent of the two-climax theory—and tried, as a man, to describe the sensations peculiar to vaginal and clitoral stimulation. "The sensations differ as much between themselves as the flavour and aroma of two fine kinds of wine—or the chromatic glories and subtleties of two quite separate colour schemes. And even the orgasms induced by clitoridal or vaginal stimulation respectively are curiously, though not widely, *different. . . .*" The original doctrine, as spelt out in Freud's *Three Essays on the Theory of Sexuality*, suggests that clitoral stimulation is the one first experienced by little girls. Adult women are expected to have made the transition from clitoral response to vaginal response; if they fail in this they may still have a clitoral orgasm but remain "vaginally frigid." Not surprisingly this doctrine has troubled many women.

Many psychoanalysts, the bulk of them men, followed Freud in viewing the clitoral orgasm as a sign of immaturity, neuroticism, masculinity (the clitoris as penis), or even frigidity.[11] Marie Bonaparte, for instance, refers to the "most remarkable biological feat" of the mature woman in being able to deflect and displace the libido of the clitoris to the "purely feminine channels" of the vagina. Similar sentiments are echoed in Deutsch, Farnham, Marie Robinson and others. An extreme advocate of the Freudian view is Bergler, who insists that every woman who does not have a *vaginal* orgasm is frigid. At the same time a number of psychoanalysts have taken issue with Freudian orthodoxy.

Physiologically there appear to be good reasons why a vaginal orgasm is unlikely. Anne Koedt[12] has pointed out that the vagina, like all other internal body structures, is poorly equipped with end organs of touch: "The internal entodermal origin of the lining of the vagina makes it similar in this respect to the rectum and other parts of the digestive tract." Moreover, the degree of insensitivity inside the vagina is so high that "among women who were tested in our gynaecologic sample, less than 14 per cent were at all conscious that they had been touched." Masters and Johnson, the American sex researchers, are widely seen as having destroyed the superstition of two distinct kinds of female orgasm.

As well as the theory of two types of female orgasm a number of other Freudian concepts can be criticized. The latency period, for example, in childhood sexuality is generally seen as an inevitable component in development of the individual, whereas it may be largely conditioned by factors of social repression. Similarly the theory of *penis envy* and the corollary idea of *castration complex* may be more sociological phenomena than psychological states through which every person must progress. Supporters of women's liberation have been quick to point out that women do not envy the penis *per se* but only for the social pretensions it gives a man.

When Freud first presented his theories he was abused in public, not merely by the theological fraternity (of whom such behaviour may be expected), but by medical co-workers. Sex was a quite inappropriate subject for serious and respectable scientific investigation. A consequence was that medical science remained totally inadequate on sexual psychology when even the most cursory observation of child behaviour would have enlightened it. Reich[13] tells of a summer semester of 1919 in which he read a paper on the concept of libido from Forel to Jung—"Except for Freud, they all believed that sexuality was something that, at the time of puberty, descended on the human out of a clear sky. 'Sexuality awakens,' so they said."

Freud's works have been banned in a number of countries, as have those of Havelock Ellis, Kinsey and other serious researchers. In some older scientific works, such as G. Dumas's *Traité de Psychologie*, in the course of a discussion of psychoanalysis, we find expressions like the following: "Freud makes certain observations which we cannot repeat here . . .;" "Freud quotes certain sexual impressions of infancy

which it is impossible to reproduce. . . ." Some sex researchers themselves find it hard to adjust to the variety of
sexual expression in human beings, and so unconsciously
help those people who wish to repress important parts of
man's nature. In *The Sex Researchers*, for example, Edward
M. Brecher sees Richard von Krafft-Ebing (1840–1902)
author of *Psychopathia Sexualis*, as portraying sex "in almost
all of its manifestations as a collection of loathsome diseases."
His major work remains today "one of the main vehicles for
spreading this doctrine of sex as a disease from country to
country and from generation to generation."

The neglect of sex by scientists, for ethical or professional
reasons, has led to the paradox that one of the most important
aspects of human psychology and physiology is heavily under-
researched. For example, from 1928 to 1963, the number of
specific references to female orgasm in *Psychological Ab-
stracts* was under thirty, and the number of references to
frigidity was under forty, an average of about one per year.
The superstitious taboo on sex, maintained by society as a
whole and by important parts of the medical profession, has
been responsible for this situation. In 1930, Van de Velde
pointed out in an introduction to his classic *Ideal Marriage*
that such a publication would have many unpleasant results
for him because of the habit of human beings to condemn
what is unusual, and for this reason he could not have written
the book earlier because of the requirements of his medical
practice.

It was long held, even in medical circles that women
have no capacity for sexual pleasure. A physician in 1883,
writing in a New Orleans medical journal, said that he did
not believe that one bride in a hundred accepted matrimony
from any desire for sexual enjoyment—though some women
from the "lower elements" of society might admit to desiring
sexual gratification.

Many authorities in medicine and psychology up to the
time of World War I agreed that sexual feelings in young
women were pathological and abnormal. Mary Melendy,
physician and Ph.D., wrote *The Perfect Woman* (1903)
without a mention of sexual satisfaction, orgasm or frigidity,

but counselled heartily against "self-abuse," a habit which could lead to paralysis, heart-disease, failing memory, insanity, and suicide. Even in many modern books there are clear efforts to minimize female sexual desire and to play up a woman's interest in children, home-making, and security.

Superstition is not "structured" into science as it is into theology or metaphysics. Where the methods of science are applied responsibly there is at least a fair chance of finding out what man is. There is hope for us in this.

CHAPTER SIX

MODERN SUPERSTITION

The folk superstitions surrounding sex, procreation, marriage, etc, have continuity from ancient times to the present. One myth with enduring currency is that a girl with a large mouth has a large vagina, and that a large male nose suggests a large penis. It is still believed that a man who drinks vast quantities of milk will ejaculate a greater volume of semen, and that a woman with a dry vagina during intercourse has been unfaithful. Such specific doctrines have survival power in society for a variety of psychological reasons, though they would be relatively easy to dispel on empirical grounds.[1]

The continuity of superstition is clearly shown in the persistence of sexual ritual, from the overall framework of the marriage ceremony to such particular matters as the use of confetti and the need to consumate the marriage on the wedding night. The association of confetti, for instance, with luck ("it paves the way") shows the persistent requirement that the forces of fortune be cajoled into favouring the newly married couple.[2] Sometimes aspects of the wedding ritual in modern society exhibit a mysterious cruelty, as when cases are ripped open for confetti to be inserted or when the sleeves of top coats are sewn up. Such circumstances, representing a type of "privileged aggression," clearly indicate the human psychological need for ritual.

A wide range of specific sexual superstitions persist. Many girls have been told that the likelihood of conception is related to the time of the two orgasms, that if man and woman respond at the same time then conception is assured.

There are still fears in some men that the vagina can clasp the penis and make a withdrawal difficult if not impossible.

There are still many funny ideas about menstruating women. One writer[3] describes the reaction of a Devon butcher following a complaint about meat that was not fresh: the butcher remarked that perhaps the cook was "in that state" when she prepared the meat. Girls are still told today that they should not wash their hair while menstruating, or pick fruit lest it go bad.

The effectiveness of various contraceptive techniques is often hampered by superstitious and silly attitudes about sex, the body, etc. Some women believe that if they forget to take their pill one night a double dose will suffice the next. There are many cases on record of where a woman, though sexually active, has taken no contraceptive pills for a week or so, and then consumed half-a-dozen to redress the balance. Nor is it uncommon for people to think that the *least* fertile time is midway between a woman's periods, a belief relating to an earlier doctrine that menstrual blood and the "woman's seed" are somehow connected. Michael Schofield, in *The Sexual Behaviour of Young People* (Pelican), records one teenager's contribution on the subject of contraception: "There's the Greek method. Apparently one can temporarily sterilize onself by heating one's organs in boiling water."

An interesting article in a recent *New Society*[4] relates how women's feelings towards their own bodies can affect contraceptive measures. Female sterilization, for instance, is an alarming possibility to many women who feel that "if you lose your womb you lose your man." In such an attitude the power that a woman has over a man lies in the womb, and sterilization (which need not involve the uterus) would undermine the man/woman relationship.

One body concept influencing attitudes to contraception, and recorded by Sheila Kitzinger of Jamaican peasant women, is the idea that there is one passage leading from the mouth down through the stomach and uterus, where it branches out to reach the anus and vagina. The women believe that anything inserted at one end of the passage may emerge through the other, and that there is a danger of blocking when, for example, a sheath is used. There are many tales of how a woman's husband used a condom which came off and passed into the passage, to gradually work its way up her throat, where it finally choked her.

Today many women still feel, partly under the stimulus of Roman Catholicism and other reactionary creeds, that contraception is "against nature." Some believe, and have been told by priests and other moralists, that artificial birth control can cause cancer, sterility and a whole host of other ills. A fifteen-year-old Jamaican girl, waiting in an English hospital (with dangerously high blood pressure and toxaemia) for her first baby, is quoted as saying on birth control, "Oh, no, I wouldn't. It's too dangerous."

In Britain we are accustomed to hearing talk of widespread sex education, the corollary being that today no-one is ignorant of the basic facts about sex. In fact much of the education given is superficial and moralistic, and in too many cases misleading or false information is conveyed to children. A recent booklet by Maurice Hill and Michael Lloyd-Jones[5] has pointed out a number of errors in sex education books written by doctors and other medical experts. For instance, Dr Julia Dawkins informs her readers (reference in *Sex Education*) that "The left scrotum hangs lower than does the right." The Hill/Lloyd-Jones comment—"We are surprised that a doctor should not know that one scrotum per man is the usual quota." Hacker states that semen is colourless and odourless. In the Dawkins book, on a diagram of the sex organs coyly labelled "his" and "hers," the urethra is labelled as the vagina. Dawkins also chooses to observe that "Your eggs won't get fertilized until you are quite grown up and have a husband."

Pauline Perry suggests that there is a fall in temperature at the time of the month when ovulation takes place. In fact there is a *rise* in temperature. Matthews notes that the sperm swim up the long tube "which runs through the man's groin and into his tummy." Thus spermatozoa somehow get mixed up with food! Sometimes the facts of genetics are equally erroneously portrayed: Hernandez writes: "Except for the sex cells, each human's millions of cells contain 48 chromosomes in pairs. But the female's egg cells and the male's sex cells contain only 24 chromosomes each." In reality there are 23 chromosomes in the egg-cell and the same in the sperm cell, making 46 altogether.

Dawkins is as confused about psychology as she is about physiology: "Sexual feelings begin to develop soon after a boy or girl is physically grown up." And many of the writers cited by Hill are quite unable to distinguish between puberty and adolescence. In one book, to cap it all, it is said to be *legally* wrong, in our society, to have sexual intercourse "before you are married" (*What to Tell Your Children About Sex*, Allen and Unwin, 1966). And in a quite absurd Catholic Truth Society pamphlet, *Sex-Instruction in the Home* (1965) by the Rev. Aidan Pickering, we are told that if children ask how a baby begins, "they are quite satisfied if you tell them that you can feel it begin." The Roman Catholic attitude, as stated by Pickering, is that sex education means training the will as a means to purity.

One aspect not mentioned by Maurice Hill in *Sex Education* is the extent to which a rampant "sexism" pervades existing books on sex education that a teenager may come across in the typical bookshop. In the bulk of such publications it is assumed that there is an ineradicable psychological difference between the sexes; little supporting evidence is ever adduced for this assumption. In an excellent article in *The Times Educational Supplement* (August 8, 1972), Mary M. Hoffman examines a number of books in this context.

Thus in *Boys and Sex* Dr Pomeroy says that he has "directed the book towards boys rather than to boys and girls because the two sexes have different approaches and attitudes which could not be readily combined in a single volume." Hoffman notes that much of the material in the companion volume *Girls and Sex* is duplicated, particularly the "Question and Answer" sections at the end of the book and, inevitably, in the parts dealing with anatomy.

There is also the effort, traditional in all sex education, to play down the importance of sex in female attitudes. Pomeroy: "Sex is less important to girls than their public image. . . . Girls in fact seldom talk about sex as sex, and

M

even when they do, they don't talk about it as boys do." Hoffman's comment: "When I quoted this last to a group of lower sixth girls in a school the spontaneous howls of derision which greeted it were such that I wish Dr Pomeroy had been there." In Pomeroy and the other writers surveyed—Kenneth C. Barnes (*He and She*), Kenneth Walker (*The Physiology of Sex*), and Pauline Perry (*Your Guide to the Opposite Sex*)—there is a mixture of unsupported assertion and downright mythology: girls are less capable than boys of controlling their sexual desire once it has been aroused; girls are definitely less modest than boys; the woman who "fights her own battles" has trespassed into a sphere "that does not by right belong to her;" sex plays a "far smaller" part in the lives of men than it does in the lives of women, and yet the "enjoyment of what may be termed undiluted sexuality may be regarded as the prerogative of the male;" promiscuous sexual activity is a sign of mental illness; boys necessarily prefer to marry virgins; the sexually experienced person is irresponsible or ruthless, etc, etc. What is singularly depressing is that such sentiments can be found in the writings of "experts," people to whom the young responsible person may reasonably expect to turn for guidance.

In the home, where the reactionaries would like to see all sex education confined, the situation is particularly unfortunate. Michael Schofield (*The Sexual Behaviour of Young People*) found that parents "are only rarely the initiators of sex knowledge" in their children: 67 per cent of the boys and 29 per cent of the girls said that they had never at any time had any advice about sex from their parents.

> We've never discussed it. My mother always says its filthy. (Girl, aged nineteen).
> I can't ask my mother anything. She just looks at me dubiously and says, "What do you want to know for?" She thinks I'm learning too fast. (Girl, aged sixteen).

Parental anxieties about sex in their children are reflected in primary school and beyond. It is almost inevitable in the present climate that the bulk of teachers see their role as sex educators as repressive and traditional. The situation is not depicted by them in such candid terms and in the majority of instances teachers are not concerned with formal sex education. However, teachers still find themselves having to instruct their charges in the use of the "appropriate" toilets, the "undesirability" of sex play, the "rudeness" of certain words, etc. This is all part of sex education and necessarily represents an unhealthy thread in the traditional approach. A. S. Neill of Summerhill writes:

> When Zoe was six she came to me and said, "Willie has the biggest cock among the small kids, but Mrs X [a visitor] says it is rude to say *cock*." I at once told her it was not rude. Inwardly I cursed that woman for her ignorance and narrow understanding of children. I might tolerate propaganda about politics or manners, but when anyone attacks a child by making that child guilty about sex, I fight back vigorously.

In 1961, Michael Duane, the quite untypical head-master of Risinghill, decided on one occasion to abandon the formal lesson and invite the class to ask him *any question*—"I will promise to answer it truthfully if I know the answer." Then he left the room to allow questions to be written down and handed in. Virtually all the questions, reprinted in an article in *Family Planning* and in Leila Berg's *Risinghill: Death of a Comprehensive*, were on sexual topics and revealed, above all, the sad ignorance in lively and energetic children. Mr Duane duplicated an uncensored account for his staff and gave a copy to the governors. An Inspector Macgowan was horrified and went to County Hall to show the Chief Inspector his copy of the document that proved that when the boys of Risinghill said "What is a cunt?" Mr Duane told them. When the *Family Planning* article appeared, without naming the headmaster or the school, the LCC at once summoned Mr Duane to County Hall to account for his behaviour! As a result of Mr Duane's humanitarian philosophy Risinghill was closed down, and to this day Mr Duane is without a school teaching post.

With misinformation and facile moralizing it is hardly surprising that many people still view sex with superstitious
dread. We tend to assume that in modern liberal society
sexual knowledge is widespread. This is far from the truth.
The magazine *Forum* was recently approached by a couple
who did not know about sexual intercourse: on their honey-
moon they had lain together motionless "waiting for something wonderful to happen," and nothing did. A small percentage of women visiting fertility clinics are still virgins:
they think that kissing is enough for conception, or that
their husbands should be able to penetrate them through the
navel. Eighteen out of one thousand patients of Dr Dickin-
son[6] remained virgins for one or more years after marriage
(the average was four years) because neither wife nor husband knew how to perform sexual intercourse. Brecher mentions the comment of one girl on her own sex education: "My
mother told me that a man plants a seed in the woman so I
thought that a man picks up a spade and puts a little dirt
on—I don't know where—and puts in a little seed, like a
geranium seed."

A degree of ignorance at a rather different level was
recently revealed by a correspondent to a glossy magazine.[7]
A woman, accustomed to fellatio, i.e. sucking her husband's
penis, often swallowed the semen and wondered whether
it might be upsetting her diet. She was assured that the
quantities of substance consumed were so small as to be
negligible as a dietary factor. Paul Ableman comments that
the substance is rich in protein, enzymes, sugar and other
nutrients, and that with a hard-working prostitute it might
"just prove to be a nutritional factor." One superstitious
theory about swallowing semen is that it may cause a woman
to grow a moustache.

One of the most widespread myths is that penis size is
crucial to love-making ability. This superstition has brought
endless misery to vast numbers of men. It has been said that
you can tell the size of a man's penis by the size of his feet
(as well as his nose), and that tall men have longer penises.
This is untrue, there being little variation in size of erect
penis from one man to another. Men have been known to

attach weights to their penis in pathetic efforts to extend it, and that male anxieties on this score are not dead can be seen by even a cursory perusal of the girlie magazines. In a letter to me (May 10, 1972) Marjorie Proops of the *Daily Mirror* cites the myth that "A man with a small penis is always sexually inadequate" as one of the sex myths cropping up most commonly in correspondence from readers (other common myths she cites relate to *masturbation,* i.e. hair will grow on palms of hands, men will become impotent, women sterile, they will go mad, etc, *breast size,* i.e. women with small breasts are poor risks in bed, *husbands* who are regarded by their wives as being perverted for liking girlie magazines, oral sex, etc).

There is a schoolboy chant that belies the importance of the large penis:

> Long and thin goes right in
> And doesn't please the ladies.
> Short and thick does the trick
> And gives them all the babies.

Most substantial evidence exists however for destroying the superstition that a competent lover must have a large penis. Much of the work of Masters and Johnson focussed on sexual performance and the associated bodily manifestations. A conclusion of the research was that a man's sexual performance is unrelated to the size of his penis. It is important that this sort of information be widely circulated. Many psychiatrists have reported that feelings of inferiority on account of penis size present serious problems for substantial numbers of men. Masters and Johnson have pointed out that a penis that is large in its unstimulated state does not increase in length proportionately during erection, i.e. short penises generally increase more, proportionately, than do long ones. One man in the study group with a flaccid organ less than three inches long experienced a 120-per cent increase in penis length during erection, until it measured nearly seven inches. Another man, with a four-and-a-half inch flaccid organ reached the same erect size upon stimula-

tion, i.e. just under seven inches. It has also been pointed
out that the vagina has some capacity to adjust itself during
sexual arousal to the size of the male organ. In the words
of Masters and Johnson, "Full accommodation usually is
accomplished with the first few thrusts of the penis, regard-
less of penile size." Nor—as we may expect in view of the
above considerations—is the size of the vagina of crucial
importance in the satisfaction of the partners. (Other myths
exploded by the Masters/Johnson work are the idea of two
types of female orgasm, vaginal and clitoral, and the notion
that a woman, like a man, is limited to one climactic orgasm
that produces satiety.)

Superstitions about penis size have featured in much
racialist mythology. White communities in contact with
coloured men have frequently ascribed vast capacities of
sexual potency to the Negro. Like all superstition the pro-
ponents have lapsed into absurdity. Mixed bathing pools
have been banned in the Southern states of the U.S. on the
grounds that white women might conceive if swimming in
the same water as black men. And the inevitable corollary
—that Negroes have large penises—has been enthusiastically
argued by white racialists, despite the paradox that such a
situation would demean white men, according to current
superstition, in the love-making stakes. Wayland Young
mentions the incredulity of an American Negro in Rome
in talking of some society women at a party—"They ask
you . . . the length of . . . your prick." And the black comedian
Dick Gregory has been quoted as attacking the desegregation
of washrooms as it ruined the greatest thing the blacks had
going for them—the myth of the giant cock.

Another area of potent sexual superstition concerns words,
particularly "four-letter" words. The aura of taboo that surrounds such utterances is quite extraordinary and can only be
understood by observing the continuity of superstition
regarding verbal utterances throughout the development of
human society. In all historic communities certain words have
been invested with magical qualities and have in consequence been prohibited or allowed only in a few tightly-
defined circumstances. It is worth glancing at word-taboos

in various societies, the more readily to comprehend the "four-letter word" neurosis of modern society. . . .

Personal names have been tabooed in many societies. Primitive man has regarded his name as a vital part of himself: the Tolampoos of Celebes believed that if you wrote a man's name down you could carry off his soul along with it, and in many primitive Indian communities today care is taken by individuals to keep their names secret. In similar fashion the Australian aborigines believe that if an enemy learns their name he will acquire power over them thereby. The Indians of Chiloe used to keep their names secret for they claimed that there were fairies on the mainland or neighbouring islands who, if they knew folk's names, would do them an injury. In many primitive communities to enquire of a person "What is your name?" is most indelicate, and immediate antagonism may be created. Frazer gives many examples of name taboos.[8]

It is not simply one's own name one must guard against. There are strict taboos on the names of relatives, the names of the dead, and the names of kings and other sacred persons. Among the Zulus, for instance, no-one was allowed to speak the name of the chief of the tribe. In the tribe of the Dwandwes there was a chief called Langa, which also means the sun; hence the name of the sun was changed from *langa* to *gala*, which it remains to this day. Similarly the names of gods were tabooed, and to utter such a name was thought to bring all manner of disaster on the tribe.

In such a fashion have words come to acquire a magic significance. Simply to say them aloud fills the primitive man with unbearable anxiety. Are we so different today? Why do so many people throw up their hands in horror when they hear a word they consider obscene? It is quite remarkable what effect a mere sound on the air can have. People rush for their pens to write stern letters; television producers have to account for their actions; respectable newspapers run discussions on the possible effects of "indecent language." For a person to pronounce certain syllables (or, more usually, just one) stimulates a veritable orgy of promiscuous wrath. When Ken Tynan said "fuck" on television this trivial event was discussed in press leaders and even recorded in a subsequent novel (Richler's *Cocksure*).

In many primitive communities no-one is allowed to write down certain words. There is a close parallel in modern society. The trial of Lady Chatterley was initiated largely, because author and publisher had seen fit to record "obscene" language. Nor can modern dictionaries steel them-selves to print the more obvious "four-letter words"—*fuck, cunt, cock, arse, shit, piss, fart,* etc. *Fuck,* for instance, has been banned from all general dictionaries ever since the eighteenth century. Weekly, in the *Etymological Dictionary* (1921), makes no reference to it, nor does H. L. Mencken fourteen years later in his epic *The American Language.*

There was a time when *fuck* could appear. It is faithfully recorded in John Florio's Italian-English dictionary, *A Worlde of Wordes* (1598) and it also appears in Skinner's *Etymologicon Linguae Anglicanae* (1671). In 1721 Nathaniel Bailey defines it as "to lie with a woman," and nine years later added to the definition in his *Dictionarium Britannicum* —"a term used of a goat." By 1775 John Ashe is describing the word as *low* and *vulgar,* and in 1785 Francis Grose could only manage to identify the word by its first and last letters (an emasculated *fuck* vis: f**k, evidently loses some of its magic power). This is in fact a device employed in some of our national newspapers.

The Oxford University Press, until 1972, refused to have anything to do with four-letter words, either in the *Oxford English Dictionary* or elsewhere. In the third edition of *Webster's New International Dictionary* published in 1962, *the* four-letter word is banned on the gorunds that inclusion would invite denunciation and boycott. We can just imagine the prudes searching through the new edition to discover any lapses. When a lady congratulated Dr Johnson on omitting all improper words from *his* dictionary he replied—"So you have been looking for them, Madam?"

So if you tend to smile at the savage who dare not utter the name of his chief, for fear of all sorts of calamities, make sure you yourself harbour no superstitions about *fucks* and *cunts.* Are you at home with such words? They are explicit and unambiguous. The heavens will not fall in if you utter them. Words have no magic power; a mere sound is hardly potent with supernatural possibilities. What about the Eskimos?! Not long ago the Canadian Government[9] wanted the Eskimos under its jurisdiction to take on surnames. The Eskimos gave much thought to this, and eventually some took a second name that fitted their description—*big man, small woman, large hands, short legs,* etc. Some I am happy to relate, took the last name *Oseeuk,* the word for a man's genitals. Not much sexual superstition in this!

The ethical considerations that surround in bogus fashion our language about sex are brought in by the moralists wherever sex is mentioned. In sex education this is particularly noticeable. Children are given many "reasons" why they should refrain from making love: they are given little advice how to become proficient lovers. The Maurice Hill booklet,[5] is an excellent exposé of some of this superstitious moralizing. It is worth quoting from the Pickering Catholic Truth Society pamphlet:

> You would be appalled to see the anatomy charts of the sexual organs and the growth of the unborn child published for use in schools with boys and girls of twelve and thirteen. . . . The problem is not chiefly of giving information, but of training the will. . . . We say nothing of internal anatomy; we use no scientific terms; we take no examples from plants or animals. . . . Instead we take our examples from the feasts and prayers of the Church, and keep the whole thing as simple and spiritual as possible.

This sort of stuff is even worse than David Reuben's explanation of why women have two breasts—"It obviously was decided that way by some higher power."[10]

With sex education superficial, anti-erotic, and obsessed with purity and prohibition, it is hardly surprising that people still harbour superstitions about sexual practice. Even nakedness is a source of worry to many people, and they go to some lengths to hide the fact of their penis or breasts. Some men are embarrassed to be examined by women doctors and many women have been known to delay a needed visit to a male physician for worry of being examined in the breast or genital area. There are still women who will not allow a male physician to deliver their babies. The nudity superstition is clearly shown by the legal prohibition of "indecent exposure:" the human body *indecent* an evident taboo that shows the sickness in modern society. I have just read a brief report in the *Guardian* (July 5, 1972): Ingrid Krause, aged thirty-four, a West German visitor to Ragusa, Sicily, has been fined 10,000 lira (£6.67) for "sitting in a public place in an attitude contrary to public decency by having the legs crossed so as to show the left thigh entirely nude."

The superstitious hostility to sex is also revealed by *institutional* attitudes. Men and women in gaol are not expected to have sexual needs, nor are people in hospital. Handicapped people suffer particularly from this sort of taboo attitude and their plight has recently been investigated for television and the press. The Swedish Institute for Sexual Research has recently called for an international undertaking to study possibilities for a normal sex-life for the physically handicapped.[11]

Dr Maj-Briht, president of the institute and a pioneer sexologist, has observed that "we lock these people up and pretend they have no sexual needs," and that "most have the same needs as we have." Charges are made that *most* people in Western society are opposed to the idea of sex for the handicapped, despite the fact that sexual drive need not be affected detrimentally in people with severe disability (sometimes drive can be intensified, as with some female paraplegics). A Dr Walan is quoted as blaming parents and the authorities for what amounts to a cruel deprivation forced on suffering people. So great is the anti-sex taboo that sign language for the deaf (at least in Sweden) does not contain a vocabulary of sex terms: young people who are deaf cannot even discuss sex. Blind people know the words but rarely appreciate what the opposite-sex body looks like. Dr Walan and her colleagues have hired live models so that the blind can discover the human body by touch, and she has

further suggested, as a final resort, that volunteers be provided for the handicapped to give them some semblance of
a sex-life.

The state of the law on sex is one of the clearest signs of
prevalent superstition. In many countries, for instance, anal
intercourse between husband and wife, with both consenting happily enough, is illegal. In *Forum* and other magazines
with advisory intentions the severity of the law on this subject is pointed out from time to time: in England, for
instance, *coitus a terge* is theoretically punishable by life-
imprisonment. In the United States almost every type of
sexual activity has been subject to legal prohibition in one
State or another, and more than one commentator has
observed that if existing law were implemented more than
ninety per cent of the adult population would find themselves
in gaol! In Boston in 1948 there were even 248 arrests for adultery and as late as 1954 the sex laws were said to receive
"normal enforcement." In South Africa there is even a ban on
sexual intercourse—between white and black. And according
to existing law in Spain, lesbians are liable to execution!

The severity of existing legislation in sexual matters is in
part sustained by the widespread view that uncommon or
minority sexual behaviour necessarily represents *perversion*.
Even where certain forms of behaviour are not illegal their
disclosure in, say, a public man is sufficient to ruin a career:
an MP or school-teacher found to have transvestite or fetish-
ist tendencies—though limited to private manifestation—
would not last long. And homosexuality, common in all
human society, is still viewed with a mixture of disgust
and amusement, and such superstitious attitudes can often
be found in people who should know better. The David
Reuben book, already cited, is a blatant case of erroneous
information on homosexuality, and the national Campaign for
Homosexual Equality felt obliged to ask booksellers to insert
a printed sheet carrying corrections. I cannot do better than
quote from the insert:

> *It is not true* that homosexuals wear women's clothes
> and adopt female mannerisms (p. 141); in fact most are

neither more masculine nor more feminine than most heterosexuals.

It is not true that all homosexual encounters are sordid and impersonal (p. 145); homosexual relations can be, and often are, as emotionally fulfilling as heterosexual ones.

It is not true that the primary interest for homosexuals is the penis, not the person (p. 145); this is blatantly and viciously untrue.

It is not true that those who combine homosexuality with sado-masochism are "the cruellest people who walk the earth" (p. 147) while heterosexual sado-masochists are "like timid children" who rarely hurt anyone (p. 187). There is no difference between the two kinds of sado-masochism.

There have been protests against the Reuben book in various countries. In Holland, for example, in January 1971, the Central Committee for the Dutch Society of Homosexuals (COC) lodged a complaint with the public prosecutor at Utrecht against the publishing company responsible for publishing Reuben in Holland. In July 1972 the prosecutor agreed that the book was very shallow, insignificant and bigoted, but thought nevertheless that it should not be banned. The publisher however, in discussion with COC, came to agree that the book should not be distributed.

Ill-informed and superficial attitudes to homosexuality are clearly illustrative of sexual superstition. Because of such attitudes the homosexual, in all modern societies, has been subject to persistent discrimination, hostility and ridicule. In 1954 the Rt Hon Earl Jowitt, Lord Chancellor of England from 1945 to 1952, declared that when he became Attorney-General in 1929 he was impressed with the fact that:

A very large percentage of blackmail cases—nearly 90 per cent of them—were cases in which the person blackmailed had been guilty of homosexual practices with an adult person ... I asked myself whether our law was wise in making it a criminal offence for two male adults to commit acts of indecency with each other in private.

The social stigma attached to homosexuality has made the homosexual particularly vulnerable to various sorts of criminal activity in addition to blackmail. Men have been enticed and then beaten and robbed, their assailants confident in the knowledge that the victims would be reluctant to approach the police. In England and elsewhere, "queer-bashing" is a frequent activity: young thugs assault a homosexual and, if apprehended, claim they had been solicited and were simply protecting their honour. In his book *Homosexuality* D. J. West has suggested that homosexuals have been convicted of, say, robbery, on evidence too circumstantial to convict a "normal" person.

In the United States police have acted as decoys to trap homosexuals. In the magazine *Collier's* for May 28, 1954 Albert Deutsch describes how policemen have accepted bribes and protection money from intimidated sexual offenders. And more than one psychiatrist has told of personal tragedies that sometimes follow vice squad interference with minority sexual activity. Where homosexuals are discovered in the American armed forces they are dismissed. Article 125 of the U.S. Code of Military Justice includes the words:

> It is unnatural carnal copulation for a person to take into his or her mouth or anus the sexual organ of another person or animal: or to place his or her sexual organ in the mouth or anus of another person or of an animal; or to have carnal copulation in any opening of the body, except the sexual parts, with another person; or to have carnal copulation in any opening of the body of an animal.

The maximum penalty for such an offence, not necessarily involving emission and with only slight penetration, is "dishonourable discharge, forfeit of all pay and allowances, and up to five years confinement at hard labour." If discovered in government employment, homosexuals are discharged. The opponents of the Truman regime alleged that the government was employing perverts: an enquiry followed with the result that ninety-one homosexuals were dismissed from the State Department. Sometimes in American courts efforts are made to discredit the sound testimony of witnesses by associating them with "irregular" sexual behaviour.

The severity of American law in this area can be seen by glancing at some of the statutes in force until at least the late sixties:

Alabama: Crimes and Offences: T14 Sec. 106 *Punishment of Crime Against Nature*:

Any person who commits a crime against nature, either with mankind or with any beast, shall on conviction be imprisoned in the penitentiary for not less than two nor more than ten years.

Arkansas: Criminal Offences Sec. 41–813 *Sodomy or Buggery. Penalty*:

Every person convicted of sodomy, or buggery shall be imprisoned in the penitentiary for a period not less than one nor more than twenty-one years.

Connecticut: Crimes. Sec 52–216 *Bestiality and Sodomy*:

Any person who has carnal copulation with any beast, or who has carnal knowledge of any man, against the order of nature, unless forced or under fifteen years of age, shall be imprisoned in the State Prison for not more than thirty years.

These examples are typical of US law on homosexual and other "aberrant" sexual behaviour. In a number of instances reform has been accomplished (the *Advocate*, for instance, the "newspaper of America's homophile community," highlights changes in the law that benefit homosexuals, e.g. "New Sodomy Law Gains in Florida," March 15, 1972, and "Law Reform Gains in Ohio," June 7, 1972). In the majority of cases the initial law reform makes provision for "consenting adults," meaning that homosexual behaviour is not *per se* illegal. However, legislative changes of this sort do not always reduce police enthusiasm in pursuing the homosexual, and convictions may be secured on grounds of "public nuisance" or "disturbing the peace."

In England, following the relatively enlightened Wolfenden Report, a new Sexual Offences Act was enacted in 1967. In the words of the Campaign for Homosexual Equality the new Act "allowed a strictly limited amount of legality to the physical expression of love between male homosexuals who had reached the age of twenty-one." However, even with this reform a number of inequalities exist between the rights of homosexuals and those of heterosexuals. CHE points out that:

(a) In Scotland and Northern Ireland sexual acts between males over twenty-one are still illegal. Two females in a similar situation have no such restriction placed upon them.

(b) In England and Wales, sexual acts are:

(i) illegal between two males if one or both are under twenty-one, but

(ii) legal between two females of any age

(iii) legal between a female over sixteen years of age and a male under sixteen years of age, but

(iv) illegal between a male of any age and a female under sixteen.

It has been argued that if there have to be sexual laws at all, they should be the same for all, and that sexual acts between consenting males over the age of sixteen should be made legal. The current situation applying to adult homosexuality is that sexual acts are illegal in the armed forces and in the Merchant Navy; homosexual relationships between two men or two women are not allowed any legal status by the state; publications that put homosexuals in touch with each other can be convicted under common law of conspiring to corrupt and deprave public morals if the court rules that the intention is that a homosexual act will result—even though the act itself may be perfectly legal; homosexuals cannot kiss, hold hands or show other spontaneous expressions of affection in public without risk of prosecution for indecent behaviour; and the legal definition of privacy for the male homosexual demands that during a homosexual act only two persons may be present, whereas for heterosexual activity there is no such limitation.

In addition to the national legal situation there is also the question of local bye-laws and the attitude of local councils. A recent case centred on the attempt to establish a homosexual club in Burnley. The Corporation was hostile to the idea and CHE claimed that attempts had been made by the Corporation to obtain local authority powers to suppress homosexual clubs. A certain Alderman Gallagher was quoted as denying that the action of the Corporation was specifically directed against homosexuals: "We made the move because we were of the opinion that we did not have sufficient power over the establishment of any type of club. A couple of jail-birds could apply to establish a jailbirds' club." This sort of remark needs little comment.

Popular superstition also has it that people should not make love until they are past a certain age, though the age is somewhat indeterminate. There seems a general consensus that youngsters just into their teens should not be encouraged to have sexual intercourse, though the reasons for this attitude are often obscure. It is never simply a matter of venereal disease or unwanted pregnancy. With such dangers removed few parents would be happy to see their thirteen-year-old daughter leaping between the sheets with her thirteen-year-old lover. It has been pointed out that Juliet (the Shakespearean one) was fourteen, and that Queen Elizabeth I had a very serious affair when she was thirteen. Mary Queen of Scots was a widow at seventeen. Perhaps Heloise was getting past it when she fell in love with Abelard at eighteen. Clearly young people should not be pressured into having sex before they want it: are we adults mature enough not to pressure them out of it when they do?

There have always been superstitions about venereal disease, one of the most dangerous being that a man could be cured of syphilis if he had sexual intercourse with a virgin. Today it is one of the standard arguments against the "permissive society" that venereal disease is increasing in prevalence, and that the only way to stem it is to return to the old standards of morality. It is worth looking at the figures for VD in more detail. For example, according to the recently published *On the State of Public Health 1970* from the Department of Health and Social Security, the VD figures do show an increase from the mid-fifties. However, interpretation has to be cautious. . . .

In England venereal disease is generally regarded as being syphilis, gonorrhea and chancroid: of these only gonorrhea has shown a marked increase in the recent past. Chancroid is now practically unknown in England, with less than a hundred cases a year since 1964. The figures for syphilis show a steady decline for women—from 3,926 in 1951 to 1,216 in 1968; the figures for 1970 show a further decrease. For men the 1951 figure was 4,506 cases; since then the annual total has averaged around 2,500, i.e. between four and five men per 100,000.

The figures for gonorrhea are less encouraging. For men there has been a three-fold increase from 1954 to the 1970 figure of 36,996 cases. And the figures for women also show a steady increase from 1951 (3,089) to 1970 (16,556). The 1970 total gives an overall incidence of 115.72 cases per 100,000 of the population. Even with this trend it means that only about one in a thousand people has contracted gonorrhea, hardly an epidemic but clearly something to be cautious about.

There are a number of reasons why many people are keen to exaggerate the size of the VD problem. There is the obvious propaganda point that can be used in a society hostile to sex. And "venereal disease of epidemic proportions" can be used in an attempt to terrorize young people into repressing their healthy impulses. One possible reason for the "VD scare" is pointed out in a recent *New Society* (May 4, 1972) by Jerry Palmer. Until the last couple of years, the chief medical officer's annual report gave the overall total for *all* patients attending VD clinics; and this despite the fact that in 1968, for example, of a total of 195,352 patients attending clinics only 48,757 had venereal disease—49,208 required no treatment and the remaining 97,388 required treatment for conditions other than venereal disease. Palmer discusses various conditions that may be sexually transmitted, and inclines strongly against the superstition that venereal infection is flooding the country because of sexual permissiveness—"The diseases are still unpleasant, but no longer constitute the kind of public health risk that they did" (he points out that in the 1890s around ten per cent of admissions to mental hospitals were accounted for by syphilis). "To infer a rampant epidemic is absurd, and to argue that 'permissiveness' is rotting the country's bodies is the mark of resolute bias."

Perhaps we can learn something from China in the handling of venereal infection. Instead of empty moralizing there has been a constructive effort to eliminate such disease. The result is that in modern China, with medical skills presumably less sophisticated than those in the developed West, venereal disease is virtually non-existent. Dr J. H. Horn[12] has written of the Chinese approach to combatting venereal infection. Extensive propaganda was carried out by "anti-syphilis fighters:" posters were used and village radio and meetings. An opening talk of a propaganda worker would go something like this (in Horn's words):

> Comrades, syphilis is a disease that was bequeathed to us by a rotten society we have thrown out. It's no fault of yours if you have syphilis and no shame should be attached to it. It's only shameful if you cling to your syphilis when you can easily get rid of it. . . . Comrades, we're going forward to Communism and we can't take this rotten disease with us.

Thus China became the first country in the world to conquer syphilis.

That venereal disease could be generally conquered once and for all has been conceded by many people. Rosebury, for example (in *Life of Man*), remarks that the experts are agreed that with adequate effort devoted to the problem venereal disease could be eliminated. This is a matter of medical and social priority. Clearly we should eliminate all infectious disease in society, and venereal disease should be a high priority. This is a much more sane approach than to urge people to pretend they do not have a sexual nature.

We are also urged to believe that a rocketing rate of sex crime is another of the penalties of "permissiveness," and in particular we are encouraged to dwell on the murder of children in circumstances having clear sexual connections. The facts do not support the contention that young children, particularly girls, are under constant threat from potential sex criminals inflamed by modern erotica. In 1964, for instance, thirty children were known to have been murdered in Britain. Of these, two were unsolved murders, twenty-seven were murdered by relatives (usually the parents), and only one was known to be murdered by someone not a relative. The *British Medical Journal* has estimated that about four children a year are killed for sexual reasons, bad enough in all conscience for the people involved, but hardly a spectacular statistic for a population of fifty million or so.

Offences against children committed by strangers make the headlines, but in fact children are much more likely to be harmed by their parents or other relatives. In the Kinsey study of 1075 women, it was found that more than half who, as children had suffered sexual encounters with adults, had been approached by friends or relatives. Thirty-two of the adults who made advances to the women as children were friends of the family, nine were uncles of the children, four their fathers, three their adolescent or adult brothers, two their grandfathers, and five were other relatives. In the Hamilton study, adult relatives played an important part in the female children's early sexual experiences; in the Landis investigation, thirty-five of one hundred child violators were relatives; and in the Borman study, comprising forty-six cases, only seven of the offenders were strangers. What should a parent do in such a situation? Must the child be warned against brothers, grandparents, uncles—as well as against strangers? Any such approach to the problem would clearly be absurd. What parents should aim to do is love their children (it sounds obvious) and avoid all fuss if any explicitly sexual encounter occurs with relative, friend or stranger. It has been stressed that some children, despite supposed "innocence" are capable of inviting a sexual advance from an adult, and that children from a family lacking affection are more likely to do this. Findings discussed for the United States (*New Society*, May 25, 1972) are particularly significant. Reference is made to completion of a three-year study of cases in New York of sexual abuse of children.[13] Three-quarters of the offenders were members of the child's own family, with more than a quarter living in the same house as the child. In such instances the offence developed out of a pre-existing relationship. In about a third of the cases *the child appears to have taken an active part in the sexual experience.* This particular circumstance is taken as clear evidence of severe emotional deprivation in the child's background: in 80 per cent of cases there was evidence of child neglect, and in 41 per cent the parents had records of psychological disturbance, drug addiction and crime (11 per cent had been charged with battering their babies). A tenth of the mothers had suffered sexual assault as children, and a tenth of the fathers had committed offences of this type. It was found that the parents often played an active part in the offence against the child. A recent paper in the *British Medical Journal* (May 13, 1972) shows that instances of incest are often associated with deprived family circumstances, incidence of psychopathic traits, and other debilitating factors.

What these facts indicate is that the superstitious reaction of moral disgust and condemnation at the behaviour of the sexual offender is quite irrational, though understandable. What is needed is adequate therapy, where this is possible, in parallel with a removal of the social deprivation that makes it difficult for love to flower in the family unit. And at the same time we need an honest appreciation of the facts of human psychology—for example, of the fact that children can actually enjoy a sexual advance made to them by a stranger or an adult relative or friend.

Pornography is yet another field where superstition is rampant. All manner of evil is expected to flow from easy access to pornographic material, whether graphic or literary. I have explored this subject in detail elsewhere (*Pornography*

Without Prejudice, Abelard-Schuman, 1972), and I propose to say little here. However, it can be noted that serious investigations into the effects of pornography (studies in Britain, Israel, West Germany and Scandinavia) reach consensus in that bad effects are minimal and that a number of good effects can reasonably be expected to flow from easy access to explicit sexual material. The most detailed study of the effects of pornography was undertaken by the US Presidential Commission on Obscenity and Pornography. The final report is a detailed document, based on comprehensive research in various areas. The majority conclusions are clear. It is stated that if a case is to be made against pornography, it will have to be made on grounds other than the demonstrated effects of a damaging personal or social nature.

Empirical research designed to clarify the question has found no reliable evidence to date that exposure to explicit sexual materials plays a significant role in the causation of delinquent or criminal sexual behaviour among youth or adults (Part 3 Section II)

The conclusion to be drawn from the totality of these research findings is that no dangerous effects have been demonstrated on any of the populations which were studied.

The commission found, after a two-year investigation, that there were no grounds for the state to intervene in adult choice of reading matter, and in consequence the repeal of much existing obscenity legislation was suggested. When this sober and most detailed document was submitted to President Nixon (the Commission having been set up under his predecessor) he scorned it, uttered a few clichés about "moral standards" and "filth," and nothing more has been heard. In due course, no doubt, another body of competent citizens will reach substantially similar conclusions.

The most publicized document on pornography is the *Longford Report*, published in September 1972 (Coronet paperback). In short, this effort is a confused mishmash of prejudice, clear anti-sexuality and downright self-contradiction. The document, a poorly organized tome resulting from the reflections of many disparate personalities, is one of the clearest signs of sexual superstition in the modern world. It it claimed that wide sexual experience, varieties in sexual behaviour, and aspects of sex education are intolerable in civilized society and should be suppressed with the full vigour of the law. In one section of the report a handful of cases are cited to indicate the terrible consequences that flow from access to "pornographic" entertainment: yet elsewhere it is freely admitted that it is virtually impossible to adduce empirical evidence to show a link between access to erotic material and bad personal or social consequences. More than one reviewer has noted that the only useful contribution in the report is tucked neatly away as the fifth appendix (pp 460–98) out of seven. This appendix, by research psychologist Maurice Yaffé, is a survey of current work into the effects of pornography. We need only quote part of his concluding paragraph—"*In the present state of knowledge it is not possible to draw any useful conclusions which might be applied to this problem and related issues. . . .*" This conclusion quite nicely undermines the rest of the report.

Sometimes sexual superstition is found, not in repressive moralists, but in enlightened and progressive advocates of sexual liberation. Wilhelm Reich's emphasis on a dramatic orgasm, important only when experienced at a heterosexual level, deeply intravaginal and concommitant with momentary loss of consciousness, has led many couples to be dissatisfied with their adequate sex-lives, and forced them in fruitless search for experiences practically non-existent in our society. Some of the sex manuals commit similar blunders, urging everyone to be a sexual athlete. Obviously there is much to be said for experimentation between partners—but it should be done in a carefree spirit, with amusement and not distress when a complex intertwining of limbs does not yield the promised bliss.

In the area of women's lib (and male lib) some of the

most progressive thinkers slip into what may be termed sex
role superstition. At the beginning of Martin Cole's sex education film, *Growing up*, there are some spoken words about
women-having-babies and men-having-ideas, a boob that
Cole himself has bravely acknowledged. Germaine Greer in
her just concern for the undoubted exploitation of women
in modern society seems indifferent to the undoubted
exploitation of many men in the same society; Juliet Mitchell,
a supposed Marxist, when asked on television about the
exploitation of men, replied to the male interviewer that that
was *his* problem. It had been left to Esther Vilar to point out[14]
that many men get a rotten deal, but she too lapses into
extreme statement ("Basically a man is a human being who
works ... A woman, on the other hand, is a human being
who does not work ..."), justified perhaps for propaganda
purposes. The prize for sex role superstition undoubtedly
goes to Valerie Solanas who wrote the SCUM (Society for
Cutting Up Men) Manifesto. One quote will suffice:

> It is now technically possible to reproduce without the aid
> of males (or, for that matter, females) and to produce only
> females. We must begin immediately to do so. The male
> is a biological accident: the y (male) gene is an incom-
> plete x (female) gene, that is, has an incomplete set of
> chromosomes. In other words the male is an incomplete
> female, a walking abortion, aborted at the gene stage. To
> be male is to be deficient, emotionally limited; maleness is
> a deficiency disease and males are emotional cripples.

About menstruation, sex roles, language, the magic of pictures, the supposed evils in harmless sexual indulgence, there
is continuity between old sexual superstitions, detectable in
the simplest and most savage communities, and modern
sexual superstitions, easily discernable in developed industrial
societies. We still hold up our hands in horror when there
is no need; we still confuse our priorities; we still believe
that specific cause/effect relationships exist where in fact
they do not. We are still immensely superstitious about sex.

We view it with a tantalized anxiety, unable to ignore it, yet equally unable to come to terms with it.

A persistent superstition in most societies is the absolute sanctity of the marital bond. The importance of this relationship, in the appropriate circumstances, cannot be denied. However, the superstitious element is discernible in hostility to divorce, condemnation of extra-marital sexual activity, experiments with multi-person sexual relationships, etc. One attempt to break away from this sort of superstition is via "mate-swapping", an arrangement which, grounded in the accord of all the people concerned, is designed to introduce elements of flexibility and variety into individual lives.

The psychologist Albert Ellis takes an indulgent view of mate-swapping if the husband and wife are "bright enough" to handle it, and reports that in twenty years of counselling he has heard of many more reports of swapping in the past five years than in the preceding fifteen. Couples have even asked him if he knew of other married people who might be interested in a swapping episode. He suggests that as far as the US is concerned the big centre for mate-swapping is on the West Coast.

A reporter for *The San Francisco Chronicle*, Paul Avery, and his wife Emily spent two months in 1964 looking into mate-swapping in California. They met a hundred couples who admitted to being mate-swappers. Most of the couples preferred to call themselves "swingers," and boasted of their broad-minded attitude to life. The Averys drew attention to a publication called *The Chronicle* that carried ads for swappers, e.g.:

Attractive couple in late twenties, bored with conventional friendships, wishes to meet with couples or singles to exchange unconventional experiences in the unusual/exotic/unique. Both bored.

This particular ad produced three hundred replies, about a hundred from married couples.

A point that more than one writer has noted is that the swinging scene varies widely from one part of the US to another. Thus practices in Los Angeles differ in important respects from those in San Francisco, and there is similar variation in the New York or Chicago scene. Brecher, in *The Sex Researchers,* sees the scene within each city as "composed of a variety of contrasting subscenes."

In 1965 Mrs Carolyn Symonds, a nudist practitioner with her husband, decided that swinging would make an excellent topic for her master's thesis in sociology at the University of California at Riverside. Her thesis, based on extensive research, was entitled "A Pilot Study of the Peripheral Behaviour of Sexual Mate Swappers." The paper was accepted in 1968 as partial fulfillment of MA requirements.

According to Mrs Symonds the Californian swingers belong to two distinct philosophic groupings—the *Utopian* and the *recreational.* The first group are concerned with building a better world and to this end involve themselves in commune social patterns allowing sexual freedom: some call themselves "communitarians." By contrast the recreational swingers have no long-term social aims but simply believe that it is more fun for couples to have sex together than to meet for bridge or golf.

In 1966 Dr Bartell, a young anthropologist at Northern Illinois University, carried out research, with the aid of his wife, into mate-swapping. To extend their contacts the Bartells ran advertisements of their own and frequented three Chicago cocktail lounges where swingers meet. Within a year data had been secured from 204 swinging couples. Dr Bartell concluded that the couples exhibited "inherent normality." He noted that "they were average, commonplace, and uncomplicated in almost all respects. My data are consistent with the view that, with few exceptions, men and women who are 'sick' in the Freudian meaning of the term keep away from the swinging scene." It is acknowledged that voyeurism and exhibitionism are features of the swinging scene but no more so than in the culture generally.

A further study by James and Lynn Smith, is based on detailed questionnaire returns from 503 San Francisco area swingers. The findings appeared in a book by the Smiths called *Consenting Adults* (1970). Brecher summarizes this work in Chapter Nine of *The Sex Researchers* and concludes that "Swinging, in short, is as American as cherry pie." Doubtless the practice exists elsewhere also but in general the necessary research has yet to be done.

There are signs that our sexual superstition is declining. We can discuss where previously there was an enforced silence; we know more than we did; some of us are able to enjoy our sexual art and literature. There can be little doubt that sexual superstition has a future, but there is room here for debate about its likely prevalence and impact tomorrow . . .

NOTES

Chapter One
 1. Alexander H. Krappe, *The Science of Folk-Lore*, Methuen, 1930, pp. 211–29
 2. Sir James George Frazer, *The Golden Bough* (abridged), Macmillan, 1959, chapter 3
 3. W. H. Mallock, *Studies of Contemporary Superstition*, Ward and Downey, 1895
 4. Bronislaw Malinowski, *Sex, Culture and Myth*, Rupert Hart-Davis, 1963, p. 256
 5. Douglas Hill, *Magic and Superstition*, Paul Hamlyn, 1968, p. 11
 6. Quoted by Fawn M. Brodie, *The Devil Drives*, Penguin, 1971, pp. 260–1
 7. This case, from Freud's *Psychopathology of Everyday Life*, and subsequent aspects are discussed by Gustav Jahoda in *The Psychology of Superstition*, Allen Lane, The Penguin Press, 1969, to which I am indebted.
 8. Robert Fliess, "Knocking on wood. A note on the pre-oedipal nature of the 'magic effect'," *Psychoanalytic Quarterly*, 1944, 13, pp. 327–40
 9. Judd Marmor, "Some observations on superstitions in contemporary life," *American Journal of Orthopsychiatry*, 1956, 26, pp. 119–30
10. B. F. Skinner, "'Superstition' in the pigeon," *Journal of Experimental Psychology*, 1948, 38, pp. 168–72
11. B. F. Skinner, *Science and Human Behaviour*, New York: Macmillan, 1953

12. J. W. M. Whiting, "Sorcery, Sin and the Superego," in M. R. Jones (ed.), *Nebraska Symposium on Motivation*, Lincoln, Neb.: University of Nebraska Press, 1959
13. Bertrand Russell, "On the Value of Scepticism," *Sceptical Essays*, Allen and Unwin, 1935, p. 11
14. A. E. Heath, "Probability, Science and Superstition," *The Rationalist Annual 1948*, Watts, pp. 40–1
15. Alfred Lehmann, *Aberglaube und Zauberei*, Stuttgart: Enke, 1898
16. Bertrand Russell, *On Human Society in Ethics and Politics*, Allen and Unwin, 1954, chapter 12

Chapter Two
1. Plato, *The Symposium*, Penguin, pp. 59–63
2. George Ryley Scott, *Phallic Worship*, Panther, 1970, p. 53
3. These examples are taken from J. Maringer, *The Gods of Prehistoric Man*, Weidenfeld and Nicolson, 1956
4. Julius Rosenbaum, *The Plague of Lust*, Paris, 1901, Vol. 1, p. 46
5. Richard F. Burton, *Memoires of the Anthropological Society of London*, 1865, Vol. 1, article X, p. 320
6. Bancroft, *Transactions of the Ethnological Society of London*, Vol. III, (New Series), 1965, p. 230
7. W. B. Seabrook, *Jungle Ways*, Harrap, 1931, p. 54
8. Robert C. Suggs, *Marquesan Sexual Behaviour*, Constable, 1966, pp. 151–2
9. Ernest Crawley, *The Mystic Rose*, Spring Books, 1965, p. 219
10. René Guyon, *Sex Life and Sex Ethics*, Bodley Head, 1949, pp. 145–6
11. J. G. Fraser, *The Golden Bough* (abridged), Macmillan, 1959, p. 136
12. W. J. Fielding, *Strange Customs of Courtship and Marriage*, Four Square, 1964, p. 104
13. Bronislaw Malinowski, *The Sexual Life of Savages in North-Western Melanesia*, Routledge and Kegan Paul, 1929, p. 37

14. Margaret Mead, *Growing Up in New Guinea*, Pelican, 1942
15. Raymond Firth, *Tikopia Ritual and Belief*, Allen and Unwin, 1967, p. 170
16. In *The Original Australians* (Muller), A. A. Abbie quotes (p. 201) some anthropologists who believe that the Aborigines knew nothing of physiological reproduction, and others who claim to have discovered an awareness of the pertinent physiological details
17. Raymond Firth, *We, the Tikopia*, Allen and Unwin, 1936, pp. 479–81

Chapter Three
1. George Ryley Scott, *Phallic Worship*, Panther, 1970, chapter 12
2. Magnus Hirschfeld, *Women, East and West*, Heinemann (Medical Books), London, 1935
3. Captain Hamilton, *A New Account of the East Indies*, Edinburgh, 1727, vol. 1, p. 152
4. Joseph Braddock, *The Bridal Bed*, Robert Hale, 1960, p. 69
5. Clive Wood and Beryl Suitters, *The Fight for Acceptance, A History of Contraception*, Methuen, Tavistock Press, 1970, pp. 20–1
6. Edward S. Gifford, *The Charms of Love*, Faber, 1962
7. Quoted by Ugo Enrico Paoli in *Rome, Its People, Life and Customs*, Longmans, 1963, p. 288
8. Peter Fryer, *The Birth Controllers*, Corgi, 1967, pp. 20–2
9. Hans Licht, *Sexual Life in Ancient Greece*, Abbey Library, 1932, chapter 6
10. Otto Kiefer, *Sexual Life in Ancient Rome*, Abbey Library, 1934, chapter 3
11. Oscar Lewis, *Tepoztlan, Village in Mexico*, Holt, Rinehart and Winston, 1959
12. Eskimo myth collected by Holm in eastern Greenland in 1884, quoted by Roger Caillois in *Le Myth et L'homme*, Paris, 1938, and by Ornella Volta in *The Vampire*, Tandem, 1965, pp. 49–50

13. Quoted by Charles Humana and Wang Wu in *The Ying Yang*, Wingate, 1971, pp. 85–6
14. Quoted by Ornella Volta, in *The Vampire*

Chapter Four
1. Benjamin Walker, *Sex and the Supernatural*, Macdonald Unit, 1970, p. 15
2. George Ryley Scott, *Phallic Worship*, Panther, 1970, p. 123
3. Edward Sellon, "On the Phallic Worship of India" in *Memoires of the Anthropological Society*, Vol. 1, London, 1865
4. These examples are cited with references in Edward Westermarck's *Christianity and Morals*, Routlege and Kegan Paul, 1939, p. 362
5. René Guyon, *Sex Life and Sex Ethics*, Bodley Head, 1933, p. 176–7
6. Quoted by Rattray Taylor, *Sex in History*, Ballantine Books, 1954, p. 61
7. Quoted by Clive Wood and Beryl Suitters in *The Fight for Acceptance*, A History of Contraception, Methuen, Tavistock Press, 1970, p. 51
8. S. de Lestapis, *Birth Control*, Burns and Oates, p. 121
9. S. de Lestapis, *Family Planning*, Burns and Oates, p. 202
10. Examples culled from Rattray Taylor, *Sex in History*
11. James Cleugh, *Love Locked Out*, Anthony Blond, 1963, chapter 13
12. Edward S. Gifford, *The Charms of Love*, Faber 1962, p. 88

Chapter Five
1. Quoted by Desmond and Ramona Morris in *Men and Apes*, Sphere, 1968, pp. 46–7
2. I am indebted to G. Rattray Taylor, *The Science of Life*, Panther, 1967, chapter 4
3. Dr Norman Haire *et al*, *The Encyclopedia of Sex Practice*, Encyclopedic Press Ltd, London, 1938, section 2, chapter 3

4. Charles Humana and Wang Wu, *The Ying Yang*, Wingate, 1971, pp. 67–8

5. Alex Comfort, *The Anxiety Makers*, Panther, 1967, p. 28

6. These examples are quoted in Edward S. Gifford, *The Charms of Love*, Faber, 1962

7. I owe these examples to Alex Comfort

8. There are good discussions of Acton's philosophy in: Wayland Young's *Eros Denied*, Corgi, 1968, and Steven Marcus's *The Other Victorians*, Weidenfeld and Nicolson, 1966

9. Clive Wood and Beryl Suitters, *The Fight for Acceptance, A History of Contraception*, Methuen, Tavistock Press, 1970

10. Peter Fryer, *The Birth Controllers*, Corgi, 1967, chapter 13

11. *An Analysis of Human Sexual Response*, Andre Deutsch, 1967, pp. 139–47

12. Anne Koedt, "The Myth of the Vaginal Orgasm," *Women's Liberation*, p. 37ff

13. Wilhelm Reich, *The Function of the Orgasm*, Panther, 1968, pp. 48–9

Chapter Six

1. The bulk of the foregoing examples are culled from Douglas Hill, *Magic and Superstition*, Hamlyn, 1968, pp. 34–61

2. Diana Barker, "The Confetti Ritual," *New Society*, June 6, 1972

3. John James, *The Facts of Sex*, Panther, 1972, p. 119

4. Sheila Kitzinger, "Body Fantasies," *New Society*, June 6, 1972

5. Maurice Hill and Michael Lloyd-Jones, *Sex Education*, National Secular Society, 1970

6. Cited by Edward M. Brecher, *The Sex Researchers*, Andre Deutsch, 1970, p. 161

7. Cited by Paul Ableman, *The Mouth*, Sphere, 1972, pp. 88–9

8. J. G. Frazer, *The Golden Bough* (abridged), Macmillan, 1959, chapter 22

9. *Guardian*, May 3, 1972

10. David Reuben, *Everything You Always Wanted to Know About Sex*, Pan, 1971, p. 29
11. *Times Educational Supplement*, May 19, 1972
12. J. S. Horn, *"Away With All Pests"*... *An English surgeon in People's China*, Paul Hamlyn, 1969, pp. 90–3
13. Study by Vincent de Francis, director of the children's division of the American Humane Association. Report in *Federal Probation*, Vol. 5, No. 3, p. 15
14. In *The Manipulated Man*, Abelard-Schuman, 1972